WHO IS GOD? WHO AM I?
A Guide to Unity in a Divided World

A JOURNEY LEADING TO LIFE ABUNDANT AND ETERNAL

By Jay R. Ashbaucher

Reid Ashbaucher Publications
Cleveland, Tennessee

Reid Ashbaucher Publications
Cleveland, Tennessee
https://ra-publications.us

WHO IS GOD? WHO AM I?
A Guide to Unity in a Divided World

Copyright © 2025 by Jay R. Ashbaucher
All rights reserved.

No part of this publication may be reproduced, stored in a retrieval system, or transmitted in any form or by any means electronic, mechanical, photocopying, recording, or otherwise, without the prior written permission of the author.

"Scripture quotations taken from the (NASB®) New American Standard Bible®, Copyright © 1960, 1971, 1977, 1995, by The Lockman Foundation. Used by permission. All rights reserved. lockman.org"

Cover image by Umkreisel-App from Pixabay.com

Copyright permissions can be obtained through the author's website: https://jay-ashbaucher.com

Library of Congress Control Number: 2025925931
ISBN: 978-1-7350948-8-5 pbk.
ISBN: 978-1-7350948-9-2 eBook

Printed in the United States of America
U.S. Printing History
First Edition: December 2025

CONTENTS

INTRODUCTION AND ACKNOWLEDGEMENTS 5

1. WHY THIS BOOK? 7
2. FOUR QUESTIONS FOR PERSONAL REFLECTION 13
3. GOD'S TWO BOOKS 21
4. WHO IS GOD? 31
5. WHO AM I? 41
6. BAD NEWS—WHAT WENT WRONG 61
7. GOOD NEWS ABOUT GOD, US, AND OUR FUTURE 75
8. WHAT THE BIBLE SAYS ABOUT ETERNAL LIFE 93
9. THE FEAR OF GOD AND OVERCOMING FEAR 111
10. UNDERSTANDING AND APPLYING UNIFYING FACTORS TO HUMAN RELATIONSHIPS. 141

POSTSCRIPT: WHERE DO WE GO FROM HERE? 155
SCRIPTURE INDEX 161

INTRODUCTION AND ACKNOWLEDGEMENTS

People have noticed quite a significant change in our world over the past 50 years. They've noticed that values have changed. What is good or bad and right or wrong is not as commonly agreed upon among people as it used to be. Something that the Biblical prophet Isaiah said has now become a normal occurrence. In Isaiah 5:20 he said, "Woe to those who call evil good, and good evil." Things that used to be good are now called bad, and things that used to be bad are now called good. There seems to be no standard for what is true; for what is right or wrong, and for what is good or bad. But is there a standard?

People have noticed a breakdown of trust. Being suspicious of people's motives makes it more difficult to trust people. Are people interested in genuinely helping each other, or is there an underlying greed for money and power that makes people more self-centered? Who can I believe? Who is telling the truth? This has led to a general philosophy that says, "Since I can't trust others, I must make my own truth. What is true for me is what I deem to be true." In light of what the world is becoming, can you blame people for wanting to trust themselves over others? But is there another way?

People have noticed that we live in a very divided world. People are divided over how to run a government. There seems to be much hatred and violence taking place due to philosophical differences. Churches also experience division, being split into differing groups over doctrines they cannot agree upon. Is there nothing that can unify such a divided world? Some who think about this have their answers. One recent answer for a better world is AI, artificial intelligence. The hopeful thinking is that plugging into AI can set us straight and fix the world. But is there another answer that will fix the world?

Seeing that the people of this world are hurting and fearful leads me to write this book. I want to help hurting people and give them hope. Disturbed and concerned over the direction of our world, I too have been thinking about the answer to what would unify all things. I write because there is an answer to this dilemma of a broken and divided world.

I believe there is a God who created this world and who cares about it. As a start to turning our lives and world around, we can plug into humanistic answers, like artificial intelligence, or we can learn about the Creator God, and who God says we are. There is an age-old philosophical problem called "Unity in Diversity" that seeks an answer to what it is that unifies a diverse and divided world. I have come to see that the God who created all things is also the unifier of all things. You can agree or disagree, but are you open to hear?

I am grateful for all of you whom God has brought into my life. None of us would be who we are without family, educational experiences, the books we read, and friends along the way. Who we hang out with has a lot to do with who we become. Very influential in my life has been the seminary training I received at Trinity Evangelical Divinity School, where I learned much about the God of the Bible and the many worldviews that exist. Especially important has been hanging out with God, and with my wife Connie. Having lived with my wonderful wife for over 57 years has considerably shaped who I am for the better. Of course, my personal friends, my church family, and many small groups, have been very instrumental in helping me see more of God and who I am. God has used them to help me work through many struggles and imperfections that needed overcoming in my life. All of you have been important people in my life, encouraging my ongoing growth in a God-centered faith, love, and hope. I am truly thankful for my recent friends, and for all of my lifelong friends and companions whom God has brought into my life. Also, without the expertise of my brother Reid, I would not have been able to produce this book. Thank you.

Chapter 1

WHY THIS BOOK?

Here is the purpose of this book, stated as briefly as I can make it: *"Unity in our personal lives and world is achieved by understanding and participating in diversity."* Huh? What does that mean? What that means is what I hope to get across in this book. We live in a divided world. To enable us to overcome the things that cause us to be divided, we need to apply what I call "unifying factors." Following are reminders of some of the things that make us a divided people and world.

OUR DIVIDED WORLD

When we pay attention to the world we live in, we see and experience things that are hurtful. Something inside of us says, "life should not be this way. Something is wrong. Something is not good and needs fixing. What do we see that needs fixing? For one thing, we see and experience in our world that unifying factors leading to oneness, peace, love and harmony are missing. Instead, we see brokenness and division everywhere. Our world is torn apart by war between nations. Governments are divided, affecting their country's well-being. Societies experience violence and crime among citizens. Marriages have conflicts and divorces over abuses or irreconcilable differences. Family members have quarrels with other family members. Neighbors can't get along. Kids feel bullied and unaccepted by their peers in school and at play. Many experience conflicts at work. We even find ourselves lacking peace and oneness with nature, for it gives us unwanted diseases, destructive storms, dangerous animals, and inescapable death. This book is born out of a desire to see the world healed from its wrongful sufferings. Sadly, unifying factors are missing.

WHO IS GOD? WHO AM I?
OUR DIVIDED RELIGIOUS CIRCLES

Christian churches are divided by differing teachings and beliefs. I have personally experienced the negative effects disunity causes in churches. I am not saying that unity means every church should believe the same things. Nor am I saying there is never a time to leave a church for the right reasons. Neither am I saying that churches should never have disagreements among their members. You've probably heard the saying that "there are no perfect churches and if you find one, don't join it or you will ruin it" (Lol). I pastored a church which was made up of persons from all kinds of backgrounds and beliefs. I can remember saying to God, "How can you bring people with such diversity and differing beliefs together in one place, and expect unity?" What I am saying is that when there is division between churches, and within churches, there are Biblical principles, what I call "unifying factors;" that are likely not being followed. "People problems" will always occur, but I have found that when unity is a priority, with God's Spirit guiding and leading us, unity is achievable, and it is a beautiful thing.

In recent years, church attendance in Western culture has been declining. Reasons may include hypocrisy, divisiveness, bad experiences, judgmentalism, power and control issues in the leadership, and lack of trust in the organized church. People have interest in spirituality, but not church. There is hope that things may turn around. One of my grandsons, together with friends, attended a Christian revival at Asbury University in Wilmore, Kentucky, in 2023. He told me all about it and some of the marvelous things he experienced. The revival went viral throughout the United States and beyond. I believe young people are recognizing things about this world that they know are not right. This could be a hopeful sign that many today are seeking answers, including who is God and who am I. Where is true life to be found? The church is the body of Christ. Jesus attracted thousands of people to him when on earth. If the church is his body, I ask myself, why are people not attracted to the church that is supposed to represent him? What is missing?

WHY THIS BOOK?

OUR DIVIDED PERSONAL LIVES

Within our inner lives as individuals, we are haunted and damaged by things like poor self-identity, guilt, anxiety, depression, loneliness, fears, self-centeredness, addictions, dishonesty, disappointments, and confusion about our roles and purpose in life. It can be hard to find a life occupation that satisfies and fulfills who I am or want to be. Many of us carry baggage into adulthood from dysfunctional upbringing. Perhaps we were affected by physical, verbal, or sexual abuses. To be happy we turn to things like material possessions, drugs or alcohol, good sounding philosophies, religions, sexual pleasures, money, power, or fame. Why do we as individuals try to satisfy our longings in ways that we find don't work? Often, we can't trust others, so we try and make life work by relying on ourselves to control how things go. What's missing?

A DIVIDED WORLD IS NOT AN EASY FIX

All the divisiveness stated above is not to say there is no goodness or beauty in the world, or no positive things happening in our personal lives and world, or in the churches around us. Nor do I wish to throw a damper on the positive thinkers out there. I would simply have us acknowledge the truth that there are wrongs and evils at work in our world, and those things hinder or prevent loving relationships, unity, and peace. I am sure it's been like this for generations throughout history. Think about this question: "Is there anything that will fix the world and make possible the good life we long for?" What would your answer be? Can your answer guarantee the harmonizing of all things, including nature itself? I'm sure there are people and movements in this world believing that "if everyone would do it my way, all would be good."

We live in a world of death, do we not? Death means being separated from life. A great way to destroy a unified life and world is to cause division. Division destroys oneness. Division causes disunity and leads to the death of relationships and to death itself. It is clear to observant and well-meaning people we live in a divided world, a world

WHO IS GOD? WHO AM I?

lacking in unity and oneness. To escape the world of death, we must discover what is hindering a true and unified life and take a journey that all must be on if we want to live.

WHAT IS NEEDED?

If everything in this present world is corrupted and dies, does that mean all is separated from its source of life, and that is why all things die? To experience life instead of death means being restored to wholeness. Wholeness means to experience oneness within ourselves, oneness with others, and oneness with nature. We must become one with a source that can restore genuine life, happiness, and peace to the world. What is life's source? Most believe that only an all-powerful and good God could restore all things to a unified whole. Is there an original Creator and giver of life, and if so, how do we get connected to such a source? We must take a journey that enables us to overcome a divided world. We might compare or liken such a journey to being in a car traveling to a desired destination. We don't know how to get there. Knowing that we sometimes have a tendency to get lost, we may wonder if we are still on the right path. Or we want to know how far we still need to go to get there. Have you ever traveled on a highway with rest stops? Oftentimes there is a map posted on the wall. You look at the map, and it has an arrow with the words "You are here." This helps to reassure us we are on the right path to where we want to go, and how far we still have to go to get there. Similarly, on a journey from death to life, if we want to know we are on the right path, and not wandering off in a wrong direction, we need to know who God is and who we are.

Many who read the Bible, will read that God has a plan to save this hurtful world by recreating a totally good world. No matter what you may believe or not believe about God, there are two questions every human being needs to answer. "WHO IS GOD? WHO AM I?" Knowing there is a God, and knowing who God is, and who I am, is essential for three reasons: (1) for the healing of hurts we are experiencing in this life due to divided relationships; (2) for rising above personal issues like fears, anxieties, character defects, and other

WHY THIS BOOK?

troubles that often confront us, and (3) for gaining a guaranteed life in God's promised good world to come. Information and exercises throughout this book will assist a person in moving forward toward answering these two life-changing questions. The result will be to discover a truly abundant and eternal life, a life of unity and wholeness in the midst of diversity.

On almost every page of the Bible we find people who are involved in some kind of a relationship with God. By using questions, one can discover what each of these person's relationship with God is like. Here is an example of the kinds of questions to ask: What are those involved in an encounter with God concerned about? What do they want from God? What do they know or believe about God? Is God helping them, and if so, how? From their experiences, what do you observe that they learned about God? Can you identify with those people and their experiences with God? If so, how? Those questions can be used for each situation in Biblical studies involving people's encounters with God. In Chapter Two, titled "FOUR QUESTIONS FOR PERSONAL REFLECTION," under question number 3, you will have your first opportunity to practice asking and answering questions concerning two kings who encounter God.

WHY THIS BOOK?

I came across the following quote attributed to Parker Palmer in his book, "Let your Life Speak." Palmer said, *"Before I can tell my life what I want to do with it, I must listen to my life telling me who I am."* Sometimes we hear words, like this quote, that catch our interest and cause us to think more deeply. When I think about the possibility of a God who breathed His breath of life into mankind (Genesis 2:7), I say to myself, "I must discover this Creator and let Him be the source of my life, telling me who I am, then I can know the direction my life needs to take."

Chapter 2

FOUR QUESTIONS FOR PERSONAL REFLECTION

One: What comes to your mind when you hear the word "God"?

Every person has beliefs, thoughts, or opinions about God. What are your views about God? Is God a person, an energy force, visible, invisible... what? What is God like? Is he kind, cruel, loving, close, distant... what? A person's "God" is who or whatever is the top authority in one's life. "God" is what or who influences us the most. Different religions have differing views of God. There are lots of "isms":

Buddhism—Siddhartha Gautama, known as Buddha (enlightened one)—we are to live by his teachings.

Hinduism—one supreme god, many gods, and goddesses—salvation is release from reincarnation cycles.

Deism—God created all things and left them to run themselves. The belief of many American founders.

Atheism—the belief that there is no God.

Agnosticism—there could be a god but, do not know for sure.

Pantheism—all in the universe, including humans, is an extension of an impersonal spirit—we are God.

Animism—primitive beliefs in various spirits that can help or hurt us, often controlled by witchcraft.

Islam—no God but Allah, belief in any other God is sin. One's destiny is determined by good deeds over bad.

WHO IS GOD? WHO AM I?

Mormonism—3 gods—father, son, holy spirit—shares similar terms as the Bible but defines the terms differently.

Judaism—the Only supreme God is revealed in the Old Testament. God has given us His Laws to obey.

Meism—I am my own God; I decide my own truth and how I will live my life.

Christianity—Christ Jesus is one with God. He provides the best explanation of both God and humanity.

Two: Why are there so many differing views of God?

Is the concept or idea of a god inherent in humans? It would seem so since most people in this world have an idea within them that there does exist a "God" or "gods." Sigmund Freud (1856-1939), founder of psychoanalysis, in his book, "The Future of an Illusion" (1927)[1], gives us a psychological viewpoint. Recognizing that people have beliefs in a God or gods, Freud tells us why. He says that nature (the world around us) is scary because it threatens people's lives. We are subject to things like earthquakes, floods, storms, diseases, and the reality of death. Humans are weak and helpless in the face of these things. Thus, they call on beings greater than themselves to help them overcome the terrors causing their fears and sufferings. Freud believed humans created these ideas of gods for self-protection from nature's forces against them. Freud called religious ideas wish-fulfillments, or illusions. Belief in gods are ways we humans have devised to deal with our need for comfort, hoping there is a moral order to the universe and an afterlife. There is truth in what he says, and I encourage you to read his total argument to understand it properly. What do you think? Is God

---

[1] Sigmund Freud, "The Future of an Illusion" (Revised Anchor Books Edition: Double Day and Company, Inc., Garden City, New York, revised and newly edited by James Strachey, 1964), read pgs. 20-53.

only real in our minds, or is there a real God? And if so, who or what is the supreme being in whom many people believe?

Is Sigmund Freud correct in his analysis of people's made-up religious beliefs involving gods; beliefs that have been passed down to them from their cultural influence? I think, in part, that he is correct. People and cultures have invented gods whom they want to believe in to help them overcome the life-threatening realities of the world around them. There is a need for a higher power than humans to save them. However, I think it is dangerous to dismiss the existence of one supreme and only God. The need for God is real. Humans do not have the ability in themselves to overcome death, nor can they create a peaceful and loving world apart from a God who promises such things. People will set up for themselves some kind of God or gods who will meet needs in their lives that are greater than they themselves can meet. It has thus far in human history not worked to think humans, through science, governments, or personal willpower, can save themselves from the wrongs of this world. A new development in our world is something called "artificial intelligence." Some believers in AI think we need to create a new world religion that all people on earth can ascribe to. One thought is, "Let's use AI to reprogram the Bible. Out with the old and in with the new." That's why the two questions proposed as the subject of this book are vital; Who is God? And Who am I? Is it possible that the God of the Bible who created this world really exists, and that the reason people invent their own gods is because they reject, or are ignorant of the God who truly is their Creator? After reading Romans 1:18-25 and Acts 17:22-31, what do you think?

Three: Why is it important to know who God is?

It matters because our life is shaped by the God we believe in, or don't believe in. Our view of God answers questions such as the meaning of life, our purpose, our reason and motivation for living, our hope for the future, and our final destination. Differing views of God result in different views of the world, and in conflicting ideas of an afterlife and how to get there.

WHO IS GOD? WHO AM I?

Furthermore, it's important to know who God is because knowing God determines who we are. Our self-identity comes from our God. Have you ever heard people offer excuses for their bad and imperfect behaviors by saying, "We are only human, we are not God"? People think that being human means we are not expected to be perfect like God. That is both true and not true. Jesus, who came to earth, explains God to us (John 14:9), and is our role model for what it means to be truly human. According to the Bible, being human is a person created in the image of God, a person who is created to be like God. We all fall short of who God created us to be, but that does not mean we can use our humanness as an excuse for allowing our wrong behaviors and attitudes. According to Jesus, our true humanity can be restored again. Becoming the person God created us to be is God's goal (read Matthew 5:48; Romans 8:29).

In the first chapter of this book, we mentioned that on almost every page of the Bible you will find people who are involved in some kind of a relationship with God. In the following scriptures, you will read about Hezekiah (a Judean king) vs. Sennacherib (an Assyrian king). By taking time to analyze the two kings and their relationship with God, or lack thereof, we find examples of why it is important to know who God is and who we are. For your convenience I have printed the Biblical text to save time looking it up, but in the future, you will have to look up the texts in your Bible to answer the accompanying questions.

Here is 2 Kings 18:28-35:

> Then Rabshakeh stood and cried with a loud voice in Judean, saying, 'Hear the word of the great king, the king of Assyria. Thus says the king, Do not let Hezekiah deceive you, for he will not be able to deliver you from my hand; nor let Hezekiah make you trust in the LORD, saying, The LORD will surely deliver us, and this city will not be given into the hand of the king of Assyria.' Do not listen to Hezekiah, for thus says the king of Assyria, 'Make your peace with me and come out to me, and eat each of his vine and each of his fig tree and drink each of the waters of his own cistern, until I come and take you away to a land like your own land, a land

FOUR QUESTIONS

of grain and new wine, a land of bread and vineyards, a land of olive trees and honey, that you may live and not die. But do not listen to Hezekiah when he misleads you,' saying, 'The LORD will deliver us.' Has any one of the gods of the nations delivered his land from the hand of the king of Assyria? Where are the gods of Hamath and Arpad? Where are the gods of Sepharvaim, Hena and Ivvah? Have they delivered Samaria from my hand? 'Who among all the gods of the lands have delivered their land from my hand, that the LORD should deliver Jerusalem from my hand?

2 Kings 19:14-20; 32-37 reads:

Then Hezekiah took the letter from the hand of the messengers and read it, and he went up to the house of the LORD and spread it out before the LORD. Hezekiah prayed before the LORD and said, 'O LORD, the God of Israel, who are enthroned above the cherubim, You are the God, You alone, of all the kingdoms of the earth. You have made heaven and earth. Incline Your ear, O LORD, and hear; open Your eyes, O LORD, and see; and listen to the words of Sennacherib, which he has sent to reproach the living God. Truly, O LORD, the kings of Assyria have devastated the nations and their lands and have cast their gods into the fire, for they were not gods but the work of men's hands, wood and stone. So they have destroyed them. Now, O LORD our God, I pray, deliver us from his hand that all the kingdoms of the earth may know that You alone, O LORD, are God.' Then Isaiah the son of Amoz sent to Hezekiah saying, 'Thus says the LORD, the God of Israel, Because you have prayed to Me about Sennacherib king of Assyria, I have heard you. ... Therefore thus says the LORD concerning the king of Assyria, 'He will not come to this city or shoot an arrow there; and he will not come before it with a shield or throw up a siege ramp against it. By the way that he came, by the same he will return, and he shall not come to this city, declares the LORD.' 'For I

WHO IS GOD? WHO AM I?

will defend this city to save it for My own sake and for My servant David's sake.' Then it happened that night that the angel of the LORD went out and struck 185,000 in the camp of the Assyrians; and when men rose early in the morning, behold, all of them were dead. So Sennacherib king of Assyria departed and returned home, and lived at Nineveh. It came about as he was worshiping in the house of Nisroch his god, that Adrammelech and Sharezer killed him with the sword; and they escaped into the land of Ararat. And Esarhaddon his son became king in his place.

QUESTIONS: Slow down. Search the above scriptures and think.

(1) How and why does Hezekiah seek God?
(2) What did Hezekiah know about God and what did the Assyrian king not know about God?
(3) How would you describe what each king's relationship with God is like?
(4) What can be learned about God from the encounter these two men had with God?
(5) Is there anything in this account that can be applied to who I am?

No single passage in the Bible tells us all we can or need to know about God. In reading the scriptures, questions may arise in your mind. Having read about these two kings, have any questions arisen in your mind? Keep in mind that our questions may often be answered later in life, or in other parts of the Bible.

Four: Can we know who God is and what He is like?

No one can come to know who God is if that God hasn't spoken into our world, revealing who He is. God spoke into the world of the two kings we just read about. One of the things we learn from the Bible is that there are many ways God speaks to people. It could be through dreams or visions or sent messengers or personal appearances. God has made Himself known in many ways, but primarily and most

FOUR QUESTIONS

consistently, He makes Himself known in two ways: through a written book, the Bible (Deuteronomy 31:24-26; 2 Timothy 3:14-17), and through nature which includes people (Romans 1:19-20; Hebrews 1:1-2). Take a moment to read the preceding four scriptures. From them we can learn things he deems important for us to know. We come to know God, not only from information he gives us about himself, but more importantly, by experiencing a personal relationship with him and practicing what he wants us to be and do.

Admittedly, we Christians differ in our knowledge of who God is, and then argue over who is right. Why is that? Do we think we know everything? If we Christians differ among ourselves, we might do well to listen to those who disagree with us. They may have seen pieces we have missed that could add to a more complete view of God. Certainly, the scriptures have more to give us. As we proceed to chapter three of "WHO IS GOD? WHO AM I?" we shall focus on God's two books as His primary means of revealing Himself.

Chapter 3

GOD'S TWO BOOKS

"WHO IS GOD? WHO AM I?" is a book about a journey of discovery leading to adventure. The discovery is finding out "Who is God?" and "Who am I?" All of us would do well to discover that there is an eternal life which comes as a result of knowing God. The adventure is in living out God's eternal life. It is an adventure filled with discovery, intrigue, mystery, wonder, and awesome beauty, but also an adventure filled with opposition that one must overcome. It's not an easy path. It's a process of continued learning and growing, which at times involves heartache and pain. In the end, a promised glorious completeness is reached. Although God's future glorious ending is not a fairy tale, it's like the ending in many human-made fairy-tales, "And they lived happily ever after."

How do we come to experience God and His life within us? Over 2000 years ago, a man named Jesus made the claim, "I am the way the truth, and the life" (John 14:6). It is Jesus who said, "I am the door; if anyone enters through me, that person will be saved…I came that they may have life, and have it abundantly" (John 10:9-10). What is that life? It is life that promises to one day free us from all evil. It is life that experiences the love of God. And even though this life also encompasses sufferings, it is a life that brings peace with oneself, with others, with God, and with nature. It's a life of letting God guide you. Such a life requires knowing who God is and who we are becoming. Thus, let us begin here where question 4 of the previous FOUR QUESTIONS FOR PERSONAL REFLECTION left off; "Can we know who God is and what He is like?" The answer is "Yes." And God has revealed Himself to us primarily through two books.

WHO IS GOD? WHO AM I?
GOD'S TWO BOOKS

I read a book by Kenneth J. Howell titled "God's Two Books." [2] Many people, if not most, have heard of God's book known as "The Bible." It holds the claim of being the most published book in the world. God's other book is the world God created, the world in which we all live. These two books, (1) God's holy writings, and (2) nature itself, are the primary resources God uses to enable us to discover "Who is God?" "Who am I?", and the meaning of God's kind of life, a life of eternal love. The Bible is God's history book from the beginning to the end of this world as we know it. For example, without the Bible, we would know little or nothing about the person of Jesus Christ. It is absolutely essential that we know about Jesus. Jesus is the central figure in the Bible and in world history. Again, to reiterate, on nearly every page of the Bible we find people who, in some way, are experiencing God, or a lack of. Their relationship with God, or lack of a relationship, will determine their future and their ability to experience victory over the problems they are facing. Nature too is an important book, as will be demonstrated in this chapter.

Most of us are not in the spotlight of world history. We are common people who quietly live our lives working to provide and care for ourselves and our families, helping others as opportunity affords, and enjoying the pleasures of God's created universe. No matter our station in life, our lives are important. Like the people we read about on the pages of the Bible, we matter to those around us and we can be change-agents to help the world become a better place. Like the characters of the Bible, we can use God's input to enable us to live right and have hope for the future. We might ask, "Is there any hope for freedom from the problems and evils that destroy our lives? Yes! And it's discovered in what we receive from God's two books. In reading these two books, many of us will likely have questions we can't answer. We may never know the answer to some of our questions, but from these two sources

---

[2] Kenneth J. Howell, "God's Two Books" (University of Notre Dame Press, Notre Dame, IN, 2002)

GOD'S TWO BOOKS

we can gain the needed information about God, ourselves, and what it takes to experience God's life-giving helps.

APPRECIATING THE EXISTENCE AND VALUE OF GOD'S TWO BOOKS

The existence and value of God's two books is clearly pointed out by a famous Biblical Psalm writer named David. He mentions God's two books and how our lives can be changed through them. Psalm 19:1-6 is about God's creation (nature), and Psalm 19:7-14 is about God's written words (the Bible). It's time to slow down again, do some meditating, and make some discoveries by thinking and answering a few questions.

THE VALUE OF NATURE

Read Psalm 19:1-6. What is the writer clearly claiming in Psalm 19:1? Read Romans 1:18-21 to expand on this subject. What things do these verses in Romans clearly say about God and nature? Why do you think the Psalm writer tells us about nature? In Psalm 19:4-6 we read about the sun. Think about it. How does the sun bless us? What do you think the blessings of the sun tell us about God? By observing the natural world around us, we learn something about who God is. For example, consider this. Do you see that things on this earth are made for our benefit—water, oxygen, sun, fruit trees, beauty, minerals, etc. This tells us the planet was created to be inhabited by living creatures, especially humans (Isaiah 45:18), and that the Creator cares about us by providing for our needs (Matthew 6:26-32).

HOW GOD'S BOOK OF NATURE INFLUENCED AN ATHEIST

In Psalm 19:1 and Romans 1:20, we are reminded that nature tells us awesome things about God. It is important to learn about nature. For one thing it supports the truths of the Bible. It is because of learning about nature that a well-known and leading atheist came to believe in the existence of a Creator God. In the Introduction of his book he states,

WHO IS GOD? WHO AM I?

"For over fifty years I have not simply denied the existence of God, but also the existence of an after-life."[3] In his book he explains how he came to believe that a God created the universe. Seeing the discoveries that modern science has made in recent years convinced him that there must be a God who designed our world. He claims to have followed the evidence where it leads. It seems the Bible is right about God speaking through nature when it says, "since the creation of the world, His invisible attributes, His eternal power and divine nature, have been clearly seen, being understood through what has been made" (Romans 1:20). If you are interested in reading about these discoveries of modern science, I recommend a book describing in great detail the amazing functions of DNA and how life is manufactured in the biological cell.[4]

HOW GOD'S BOOK OF NATURE INFLUENCED ME

Just as Antony Flew was convinced by nature that there must be a God to explain the facts of life's incredible design, I also learned something from nature that was a life-changer for me. What I learned about nature was from a college science professor who taught a class in the church I was attending at the time. He related to us the properties of light that science discovered. Light has two properties. Light behaves as a wave and simultaneously, it can behave as particles. The question is, how can it be both? It would seem that it should be one or the other. Then the professor presented his conclusion about these facts. What he said has stuck with me ever since. He said, "The truth lies simultaneously at both ends." Of course, God is a logical God and could not have two things be in direct contradiction to one another. Therefore, in God's mind, they can be reconciled and are not contradictory. One thing this statement has done for me is to keep me from drifting off into error by emphasizing one thing over another. It has helped me to respect

---

[3] Antony Flew, "There is a God: How the World's Most Notorious Atheist Changed His Mind" (HarperOne, NY), 2007, pg. 2.

[4] Stephen C. Meyer, "Signature in the Cell: DNA and the Evidence for Intelligent Design" (HarperOne, New York), 2009.

GOD'S TWO BOOKS

an often-used phrase that says, "there are two sides to everything." This helps me to be open-minded and to listen to both sides of an issue. It has also kept me from error in reading the Bible because the Bible often presents two sides of something that makes me wonder, "how can that be?" For example, how can Jesus be both God and man at the same time? Or, how can God be sovereign and at the same time allow free will? Or, how can we make people feel accepted and loved and at the same time not condone what they do? And, how can God be one God, and three at the same time? Or how can God be a God of wrath who punishes, and a God of love at the same time? I have found that if we emphasize one side of a truth over the other, things somehow get messed up in living our lives the right way. I've also discovered that believers in Jesus are often unlovingly divided over issues when they try and make scriptures fit into a one-sided view. Instead of listening to each other, people often approach an issue as "I'm right, and you're wrong." Of course, this does not negate the fact that "right and wrong" does exist, and that we must be able to distinguish between the two to avoid wrong's ill effects. Nevertheless, to know the truth is at both ends has allowed me to read the Bible with a proper balance. Receiving the Bible's seemingly contradictory truths, and seeking to understand them better, is a good practice.

A PERSONAL BENEFIT OF NATURE FOR ALL

Many people have experienced the value of getting alone with nature. Besides teaching us truths about God and life (Proverbs 6:6-11), it is good to experience nature's beauty, its sounds, its awesome workings, and its peacefulness. For many of us, being outside and enjoying the beauty and wonders of God's creation is relaxing and gives us time to think and take stock of our lives. We can get to a place of feeling humbled so we can practice and experience 1 Peter 5:6-7. When we truly know God cares about us, we will experience His peace of mind, which is one of the things God wants us to have.

NOTE: I have had people complain to me that God is not good because He created natural disasters that scare and kill people. According to

WHO IS GOD? WHO AM I?

Genesis 1:31, would God have created a world with natural disasters? What are your thoughts? Natural disasters is a discussion for another time, but is it possible nature's corruptions could have entered our world from a source outside of God? For now, back to Psalm 19.

THE VALUE OF THE BIBLE

Psalm 19:1-6 spoke of the value of nature, now read Psalm 19:7-14 which speaks of the value of the Bible. In Psalm 19:7-9, notice the following six words that tell what God's written book gives us: it gives us the law of the Lord, the testimony of the Lord, the precepts of the Lord, the commandment of the Lord; the fear of the Lord, and the judgments of the Lord. Next, notice the word that goes with each one of those six. In order they are: perfect, sure, right, pure, clean, and true. With each of those six statements, what value does God's word have for us? According to 19:10, what does the Psalm writer think of God's word? In Psalm 19:11-13, how does the writer say God's word helps him? Finally, in 19:14, regarding the Psalmist's relationship with God, who is God? And who is the Psalmist in terms of his response to God? How do you view God and His word? If you were talking to God, what could you say to God about what His word means to you and what it is doing in your heart? For example, what does "restoring the soul", or "making wise the simple" (19:7), and the other words in Psalm 19 mean for you? Is your soul being restored? Are you becoming wiser? As you think about this Psalm, and listen to God's voice, is God speaking anything into your heart? It may take some practice, but taking time to think about God's words can help us to more deeply internalize its truths, know ourselves better, and come closer to God?

To get a deeper sense of the value of the Bible as God's word, let's check out selections from Psalm 119. In 119:15-18, what is the Psalmist's attitude toward God's word and what does he pray for himself? In 119:25-28, how is he feeling, what does he pray to God, what does he promise to do, and what does he expect God's word will do for him? In 119:49-50, what does God's word mean to him, and how does it help him? In 119:92-94, why is the Bible so valuable to the Psalmist? In 119:99-104, what does the Bible give to him, and what affect does it have in how he lives his life? In 119:173-176, why is he so sure God will help him, save him and keep him? From the experiences of this Psalm writer, we can see how the word of God can be very important for all people. 1 Thessalonians 2:13 says this about God's word for all who believe and receive it, "...you received the word of God...which also performs its work in you who believe." Think about that. What does it mean for God's word to perform its work in you?

It is everyone's choice to believe what the Bible and nature tell us about God and ourselves. But we must keep in mind that to reject or ignore God's two books is to lose an opportunity for discovering God, His kind of life, and the truth about who we are. Following is a warning from God, but also a hopeful invitation.

GOD'S WARNING

God used His prophet, Amos, to tell the people about a coming famine from God. "Behold, days are coming", declares the Lord GOD, "When I will send a famine on the land, not a famine for bread or a thirst for water, but rather for hearing the words of the LORD. People will stagger from sea to sea and from the north even to the east; they will go to and fro to seek the word of the LORD, but they will not find it" (Amos 8:11-12). Take a moment to think about these verses and answer some questions. (1) What is bad about a famine? (2) What famine is God sending? (3) What are the people seeking? (4) Why do you think they want to hear God's word? (5) What is the result of their seeking?

Why God withdrew His word from them is explained in Amos. If you study the context of Amos, you will see that, like in our world today, hard times were coming upon the people. Their world was facing evil times and it would be a bitter day for all. After rejecting God for a long time, they now needed help, but God had withdrawn his presence and power from them. His word is missing from their hearts and minds. In our world today, we see an increase in divisiveness, anger, lawlessness, wars, and evil. People have little or no connection with the true God. Is there not a need in our world today for people to reconnect with God's word, to learn who He is, and how he can help us? Woe to us if such a famine comes to us.

GOD'S INVITATION

To those who want to hear from God, all is not lost. Through another of his prophets, in 2 Chronicles 15:1-6, when the inhabitants of all the lands were troubled with every kind of distress, God sent an invitation. He said, "The Lord is with you when you are with Him. And if you seek Him, He will let you find Him; but if you forsake Him, He will forsake you." Israel was a people without the God they previously had known and knew existed, "but in their distress they turned to the Lord their God, and they sought Him, and He let them find Him." If you and I believe God exists and rewards those who seek Him (Hebrews 11:6), no matter how troublesome life gets, He invites us to turn to Him and He will let us find Him. We can connect with God by using the two resources He has given us. God extends grace to seekers.

THE WAY TO USE THIS BOOK

"*WHO IS GOD? WHO AM I?*" is best used in a study with others. It is useful as a study guide for yourself, but is most helpful if doing it with others. You will find that many questions and subjects throughout the book are answered or commented on to some degree. It can be a good thing to hear other people's answers or comments to questions and subjects that concern us. It's amazing what we can learn from each other when people are given an opportunity to express their thoughts, and we are willing to listen. None of us knows everything, or we would be God. It is good to be open to being challenged about our beliefs and to allow God, if need be, to change our views. Learning from one another results in us becoming wiser, more mature in our thinking, more unified with each other in God's truths, and more equipped to help others. As you are discovering, throughout the book are exercises for personal evaluation and growth.

GOD'S TWO BOOKS

SLOWING DOWN

Slowing down means it may take you longer than you want to get through this book. You will have to stop along the way to look up and read Bible verses, to do the exercises, and to think more deeply about what you are reading. This is to enhance and deepen your understanding of God and yourself. It's taken God thousands of years to write His story for us. Certainly, you can slow down to think about all He wants us to be learning. The scriptures and exercises in this book cause us to slow down so as not to miss things God may want us to see or know, things that will help us grow more into God's likeness. In case you haven't noticed, slowing down is a needed practice in today's busy and hectic world. The importance of it is mentioned a lot on the internet. For example, here are two quotes: (1) "For fast-acting relief, try slowing down." —Lily Tomlin, and (2) "Slow down and enjoy life. It's not only the scenery you miss by going too fast—you also miss the sense of where you are going and why." —Eddie Cantor. May the journey ahead take you deeper than you've ever been into your understanding of God and yourself. And may God bless you richly as you continue to live out your faith journey with God.

THE BOTTOM LINE

As we read the Bible, we learn that God doesn't reveal himself all at once; rather, people build their knowledge and understanding of God over time, depending on when God wants to reveal more to us. Learning to know God and oneself is an ongoing experience lasting throughout one's lifetime. In reading the Bible, we want to observe how God reveals Himself to people in differing circumstances, and how those various people respond. We want to see who people become as a result of their relationship with God. As we hang out with the Biblical characters, the example of their relationship with God, and the results of that relationship, can have an impact on who we become (Proverbs 27:17; 15; Luke 6:40; 1 Corinthians 10:6-11). There is much to learn about what God is like from his two books.

WHO IS GOD? WHO AM I?

We want to deepen our personal relationship with God and to experience God's guidance for daily living. My prayer is that our personal relationship with God will be enhanced through reading God's words, slowing down to think, and answering thought-provoking questions. Also, by reading comments from others that are offered to help you think more deeply about particular subjects. My desire is that the reader can learn a way to approach the Bible so that in your own personal reading and study, you can hear God speaking to you.

I recently rediscovered a few words that I wrote years ago in the front of one of my Bibles: "Don't read just to learn things about God. To learn about God is an objective activity. To receive from God is subjective and will differ with each person. Knowing God is to enjoy a loving relationship. It involves two-way communication. He speaks; we listen. We speak; He listens. We are often short on listening."

Chapter 4

WHO IS GOD?

THE CREATOR OF OUR UNIVERSE

A good place to continue our adventuresome journey is where the Bible begins: "In the beginning, God created the heavens and the earth" (Genesis 1:1). This truth, that God created the heavens and the earth, is found throughout the Bible. A listing appears in the footnote at the bottom.[5] God told us He is the only creator of everything that exists, including you and me (Isaiah 44:24; 45:5, 12; Acts 17:24; Revelation 4:11). I have heard this question many times, "If God created all things, who created God?" Of course, the answer is that no one created God. The true God is the only eternal being who has no beginning or end (Deuteronomy 33:27; Psalm 90:2; Isaiah 43:10). Another way of saying it is that the true God is the uncaused cause of all that exists.[6] Since we are created beings, this is hard for us to comprehend and understand because we are confined to the boundaries of time and space. But God has no boundaries except what He places on Himself. This God who created everything says there is no God besides Him (Isaiah 43:10; 44:6; 45:5). Everywhere we read about creation in the Bible, God alone seems to be the Creator, not some lesser god or any other being. You can look up verses in the footnote below to see if this is the impression you get.[7]

---

[5] A partial listing of scriptures saying that God created the heavens and earth: Exod. 20:11; 2 Kings 19:15; Psa. 102:25; 115:15; 121:2; 134:3; 146:5-6; Isa. 37:16; 40:28; 45:12, 18; Jer. 32:17; Acts 14:15; Heb. 1:10; Rev. 10:6; 14:7.

[6] Christians believe God is uncaused because He tells us so, but if interested in the subject of something being uncaused, type the words "infinite regress" into your computer and check out the YouTube talks.

[7] Some of many scriptures referring to the Biblical God as the only Creator: Gen. 1:1; 2:1-4; Job 38:3-7; Psa. 33:6, 9; 96:5; 89:11; 104:24; Neh. 9:6; Isa. 42:5; 43:10; 44:6-20; Jer. 51:15; Acts 17:24-28; Eph. 3:9; Heb. 3:4; 11:3, Rev. 4:11.

WHO IS GOD? WHO AM I?

This does not negate the fact that God does consult with beings in the heavens whom He also created. Although we don't know exactly when they were created, we do know they witness God's works and help administer God's creation. For example, in 1 Kings 22:19-22; Job 1:6-12; 2:1-6; 38:4-7 and Psalm 82, God either mentions other "gods", or is speaking to other "gods." But, these lesser "gods", whomever they may be, are not seen as co-creators. The one-and-only God made the earth by His own power, and He has stretched out the heavens by His own understanding. God's prophet, Jeremiah, tells all the nations, who do not worship the true God, what will happen to the "gods" they worship. To Aramaic-speaking nations, Jeremiah inserts this verse in Aramaic, "The gods that did not make the heavens and the earth will perish from the earth and from under the heavens" (read Jeremiah 10:11 in context with 10:1-5, 10-12).

THE MYSTERY OF GOD'S PLURALITY

Who is this God who created the heavens and the earth? An interesting fact is that in Genesis chapter one, "Elohim", a Hebrew name for God, is in plural form. It is used over 2,500 times in the Old Testament, mostly to refer to Israel's God. Although the name is plural in form, it is surrounded by singular verbs, indicating that a singular God, not a plural God, is meant. It is true that the name "Elohim" can also be used for other gods, and on rare occasions for angels and even humans, but mostly it refers to the one God who created the universe. God Himself declares that "I am God and there is no other; I am God and there is no one like me" (Isaiah 44:6-8; 45:5, 21-22; 46:9). To avoid getting into a very long and belabored discussion about this, let me simply say that the name "Elohim" is plural, and although there may be gods and other beings for whom the name "Elohim" is used, there is only one God superior to them all. Through His written book this God claims to be the only uncaused eternal being who is the Creator of all things.

However, there are mysterious statements made by this "one and only" Creator causing us to wonder if there are other gods helping God create. God says in Genesis 1:26, "let us make man in our image." God

WHO IS GOD?

refers to "us" again in Genesis 3:22, "the man has become like one of us...." Who is "Us"? Were beings other than God involved in the creation of all things? Some have given the explanation that God creates in consultation with other spirit beings, and although they have not done the creating, they may have been involved in the planning. Believe what you will, but is it possible that God is a plural being, that is, does God have a nature that includes more than one person? Is God the "Us" in Genesis 1:26 and 3:22? As you read the next few paragraphs, notice who else the Bible says was involved in creating the world.

In John 1:1-3 we read, "In the beginning was the Word and the Word was with God and the Word was God. He was in the beginning with God. All things came into being through Him, and apart from Him, nothing came into being that has come into being." In John 1:14 we learn that "the Word became flesh and dwelt among us." The "Word" is identified as Jesus, who is then identified as "the Son of God" in John 1:34. Jesus, as the "Word" in John 1:1, is clearly said to be God and involved in the creation of the world. Referring to Jesus, Colossians 1:16-17 reads, "by Him all things were created, both in the heavens and on the earth, visible and invisible...all things have been created through him and for him. He is before all things and in him all things hold together." The God who created is also Jesus, the Son of God (Hebrews 1:2).

Are there any others in scripture, besides the Son, who are involved in God's creating of the world? There is one other. God's Spirit is mentioned in Psalm 104:30 where it says, "You send forth Your Spirit, they are created; and you renew the face of the ground." This same Spirit, who in Psalm 104:30 is involved in creating something and who renewed the face of the ground is also mentioned in Genesis 1:2, "...and the Spirit of God was moving over the surface of the waters." As one studies the Spirit of God in the Bible, could it be that the Spirit of God is involved in helping to bringing order out of chaos? The word Spirit can also mean and be translated as "breath." It appears that the Spirit of God gives life to people, as for example in Genesis 2:7; 7:22 and John 3:5-6; 6:63. He is also responsible for making possible the

WHO IS GOD? WHO AM I?

resurrection of our dead human bodies, dead both spiritually and physically (Ephesians 2:1, 5; Romans 8:9-11; Job 19:25-27).[8]

What or who is the Spirit of God? Is the Spirit a force? Is the Spirit a person? Jesus says God is spirit (John 4:24). This may account for the fact that God is able to be everywhere at the same time. The Holy Spirit was very active in both the Old and New Testament times of the Bible. Benefits produced by the Spirit of God are mentioned in Isaiah 11:2. When the Spirit of the Lord rests on someone, it produces "the spirit of wisdom and understanding, the spirit of counsel and strength, the spirit of knowledge and the fear of the Lord." In Acts 4:25-26 it is reported that David spoke by the Holy Spirit when he wrote Psalm 2. That David spoke by the Holy Spirit confirms the Apostle Peter's comment in 2 Peter 1:21 that "no prophecy was ever made by an act of human will, but men moved by the Holy Spirit spoke from God." In Psalm 51:11, King David is asking God not to take His Holy Spirit from him, implying that there is a Spirit from God who can be joined to a person. Jesus refers to the Holy Spirit as "He," (John 14:26; 15:26) implying that the Holy Spirit is a person, one who is separate from Jesus and from God the Father. The Holy Spirit is referred to as God in Acts 5:3-4, where the Apostle Peter said that a man who lied to the Holy Spirit was actually lying to God. 2 Corinthians 3:17 says, "Now the Lord is the Spirit, and where the Spirit of the Lord is, there is liberty." Thus, according to the scriptures, we have the Son of God and the Spirit of God linked to the Creator God, both called God and Lord, and both being involved in creating and maintaining of God's works. This one God is called Father in 1 Corinthians 8:6. Does it not seem quite possible that the Son and the Spirit and the Father" are all a part of the "Us" in Genesis 1:26 and 3:22? The Father and the Son are pretty well defined in the Bible. The Holy Spirit is more of a mysterious person.

---

[8] In answer to Job's complaints, Elihu speaks for God in Job 32-37; see Job 32:1-10) Elihu's thoughts were not condemned by God as were Job's three friends (Job 42:7). Elihu said things like "The Spirit of God has made me, and the breath of the Almighty gives me life" (Job 33:4). "If He should determine to do so, if He should gather to Himself His spirit and His breath, all flesh would perish together, and man would return to dust" (Job 34:14-15).

WHO IS GOD?

The Holy Spirit performs many acts of service, more than we could know unless we read all that the Bible says about Him.[9] The Holy Spirit seems to be the presence and power of God wherever needed to aid in accomplishing God's creative work. Thus, the conclusion from the Biblical data is that there is one God who is a plural being.

GOD IS A TRIUNE BEING (THREE PERSONS IN ONE GOD)

Who is God? God is One being consisting of three personal beings called "Father, Son, and Holy Spirit." The conclusion, which the early church of Jesus Christ wrestled with for many years, is that the Bible clearly teaches, God is one God (Deuteronomy 6:4), yet consisting of three essential persons, and that those who become disciples of Jesus are to be baptized in the name of the Father, Son, and Holy Spirit (Matthew 28:19). God is an awesome God, who in many ways is beyond our ability to comprehend. As a three-in-one being, God is complete and totally self-sufficient. But all-in-all, the God and Father of the Lord Jesus Christ who is our creator, is entirely worthy of our worship. Each of the three is God, and the three make up the one God who created all things. But what more can be said about who God is? In our reading of the scriptures, we will come across more detail of what this one God with three persons is like. Following is an exercise that helps us recognize some of the characteristics of this triune Creator God. Seven are considered.

---

[9] Much could be learned from compiling a list of the Holy Spirit's activities. Check out the many Bible verses about God's Holy Spirit: Numbers 11:25, 29; 1 Sam. 10:6; Psa. 139:7; Micah 3:8; Isa. 11:2; 63:10-14; Ezek. 37:1-14; Joel 2:28; Matt. 12:31-32; Luke 1:35; 4:1, 18; 11:13; John 1:33; 3:5-6; 15:26; 16:8, 13-14; Acts 1:8; 7:51; 8:29; 10:19-20; Rom. 8:9-11, 13-16; 15:13; 1 Corinthians 2:10-11; 3:16; 6:19; 12:7-11; Gal. 3:2, 5; 5:22-23, 25; Eph. 4:30; 5:18; Rev. 2:7, 11; 14:13; 22:17.

WHO IS GOD? WHO AM I?
WHAT CHARACTERISTICS OF GOD CAN YOU FIND IN GENESIS 1 AND 2?

From Genesis, chapters 1 and 2, I believe we can discover seven characteristics describing who God is, and what He is like. You will find verse numbers after each of the seven characteristics. Read them and see if you can agree that they describe, in some measure, who is God. One can find additional verses that apply.

One: Genesis 1:1-3, 21, 27; 2:7, 16-17—God exists before He creates, and in Him is life that does not die. Consider this question: Does the fact that man could possibly die imply that God created humans not to die?

Two: Genesis 1:3-5, 9, 24, 21-22, 26-28; 2:16, 21—God is ruler over all. He has power, and authority over His creation, including mankind.

Three: God is a relational being as demonstrated in _four_ of his many attributes:

A. God speaks—he communicates within His trinitarian self, and likewise with others. (Genesis 1:3, 6, 9, etc.; 2:15-17, 18)

B. God is love—being love, God cares for His creation. (Genesis 1:22, 29-30; 2:5-9, 20-23)

C. God is rational/intelligent—he thinks, plans, and wills to act with reason that is logical, good, true, right, and wise. (Genesis 1:14-18, 31; 2:17)

D. God manifests divine feelings. (Genesis 1:31; 2:18)

Four: Genesis 1:26-27; 2:2, 24—God is unity in diversity. He is an interdependent being, both giving and receiving from each other.

WHO IS GOD?

The name God, can be expressed in the singular as "He," but in verses 26-27, God is presented as a plural being as, "us" and "our.") God is both unity (one) and diversity (many). The human body made in his image is (unity) one body, with (diversity) many parts.

Five: Genesis 1:26-28; 2:15-17—God demonstrates a hierarchy within himself. There is an authoritative and submissive structure within Himself and His creation.

Six: Genesis 2:16-17, 19-20—God is a free-will being. He both makes choices and allows for choices.

Seven: Genesis 1:2, 31; 2:9, 25—God is a moral being. He distinguishes between right and wrong, good and evil.

Obviously, each of the above-mentioned characteristics of God can be expanded on, and they will be further discussed in chapter five. Also, they are not His only attributes. More are discovered throughout the scriptures. But for now, the above character traits will help us focus on what it means to be created in the image of God. The next section will help us understand the importance of being and knowing that we are created in the image of God.

OUR CREATOR IS A TRIUNE BEING AND WE ARE CREATED IN HIS IMAGE; WHY DOES IT MATTER?

Who I am has a lot to do with who is God because we are created in His image. Having information about this mysterious God forms the true basis for knowing who we are. The apostle Paul used the story of God as our creator as a starting point to share the message of God's salvation with persons who did not know the true God (Acts 17:22-31). Knowing God as our creator, and especially that we are created in His image, is foundational to our human nature and how we live our lives. The following story illustrates why being created in God's image is important information for persons who do not yet know God. Even those of us who already know God need to hear this.

WHO IS GOD? WHO AM I?

John and Helen Dekker, friends from the church I pastored, went to live with a newly discovered stone-age tribe of black people who had never seen a white man. Nor had they heard of the Creator God who made them in His image. At first, they thought John and Helen, being white, might be spirits instead of people like themselves. These people believed in spirits, practiced witchcraft, and sacrificed pigs to the spirits so the spirits might help their tribe instead of hurt their tribe. They always lived in fear, not only of spirits, but also of enemy tribes with whom they were in constant war. War was necessary to keep their enemies from stealing their goods and killing them.

Having earned their trust and having learned their language, one day John asked them, "What is your origin? Where did your forefathers come from?" They related how their forefathers, women, and pigs, came out of a hole in the ground far away in the east. They came to a great water and wondered how they would get across. A great snake arched his body so all could cross, and that is how they came to where they now lived. Eventually, John could begin teaching them the truth from God's word, which the people called, "God's talk." All learning had to be committed to memory, for they had no written language, and no one could read or write. John kept the lessons short. He began with, (you guessed it), the creation story. He taught them that God was their Creator and John had them memorize Genesis 1:1 from God's book. He had morning classes for a few who were interested, and between classes, they were required to repeat to others what they had learned. Another lesson he taught was Genesis 1:26, that they were created in God's image. Eventually, they came to understand that they were made to be image bearers of what God was like, and that they were to become like their Creator God. This meant changing things in their lives to conform to God's image, things like no more war, no more killing and stealing, doing good, loving and helping one another. The lessons in each class continued, along with the requirement to tell others what they learned. Seeing who God was, and who they were to become, changed their lives. They liked it. They liked not being at war. They loved learning God's ways. Eventually, even the women, who lived with the pigs, were respected, and the wives got to come and live with their husbands.

WHO IS GOD?

Later, as God's Bible teachings progressed, they learned that Jesus was a perfect human, representing what God was like. John would meet with individuals, not the class as a whole, and John would ask them individually if they wanted to commit their lives to God and receive God's son to live in them. Many started to become committed believers. All the time that John was teaching these truths from God's book; he and Helen would love them by doing good to them. For example, by helping cure their diseases with medicines. John gave them steel axes for tools to replace their sticks. And John had them work with him on projects that would better their lives. Not only did John teach them the truths of God, but he also taught them how to administer the medicines and treat one another's diseases. Helen helped in all these areas.

John never forced western culture on the people. He relied on God's truths and the Holy Spirit to convict them of wrongs so that they would want to change their bad ways and become like God created them to be. For example, one day a man came to John and said, "I think God wants me to cut my hair." John knew that this went against the long-standing culture of men having long hair. John replied, "Are you sure you want to do that? It would put you in a position of possibly being rejected by your people. The men's hair is very important to them. Why would you want to do this?" The man answered, "Because God wants me to do it." He went on to explain that men's hair is something that makes the men very proud and they flaunt it as a way to show superiority over others. He felt that God wanted him to become humble by getting rid of this symbol of pride. He was willing to go against his culture and suffer abuse for the sake of honoring God (Ephesians 5:8-10). He wanted to be a person who served others instead of lording it over others. In effect, this man was becoming conformed to the person God wanted him to be; a man restored to God's image. John was patient in letting the Holy Spirit work in believers lives rather than to try to change tribal culture into what would appear to be the white man's ways. John's motto, and God's will for his life's mission was, "Not by might, nor by power, but by My Spirit, says the Lord" (Zechariah 4:6). During the 20 years John and Helen lived among the people, thousands of tribal peoples became believers, fear and wars between tribes ceased, and the people loved and helped one another as

WHO IS GOD? WHO AM I?

God would want. It was most important to the people that they be image bearers of the God who loved and was changing them.

Later, John was helped by a writer to produce a book about his and Helen's work.[10] They were a good model for many other missionaries in how to effectively reach people who needed to hear the good news of God. Like those stone-age tribal people, we also are to be image bearers of our creator. Knowing who is God, and why He created us, will better help us to understand ourselves and the world around us. In this chapter, we learned about God's plural, three-in-one nature, and we mentioned some of the attributes of the triune God that can be learned from various scriptures scattered throughout the Bible. As persons created in His image, knowing what God is like has a lot to do with knowing who we are. We saw how this was true in John Dekker's mission work. For us to be created in God's image means we are to be like Him.

In the next chapter we shall expand on what it means to be created in God's image and to have the above seven characteristic attributes of God as a part of our human nature and lifestyle.

---

[10] John Dekker with Lois Neely, "Torches of Joy: A stone Age Tribe's Encounter with the Gospel" (YWAM Publishing, Seatle, WA, 1985,1999).

Chapter 5

WHO AM I?

CREATED IN GOD'S IMAGE

In chapter four we read that we were created in God's image. Here is how the account reads in Genesis 1:26-28: "Then God said, 'Let us make man in our image, according to our likeness; and let them rule over the fish of the sea and over the birds of the sky and over the cattle and over all the earth, and over every creeping thing that creeps on the earth.' God created man in His own image, in the image of God He created him; male and female He created them. God blessed them; and God said to them, 'Be fruitful and multiply, and fill the earth, and subdue it; and rule over the fish of the sea and over the birds of the sky and over every living thing that moves on the earth.'"

Further detail of how the man and woman were created is described more fully in Genesis, chapter two. "Then the Lord God formed man of dust from the ground, and breathed into his nostrils the breath of life; and man became a living being" (Genesis 2:7). The man was created first and lived for a while without the woman. "Then the Lord God said, 'It is not good for the man to be alone; I will make a helper suitable for him'" (Genesis 2:18). "The Lord God fashioned into a woman the rib which he had taken from the man, and brought her to the man" (Genesis 2:22). "The man said, 'This is now bone of my bones, and flesh of my flesh; and she shall be called Woman, because she was taken out of Man'" (Genesis 2:23). Finally, God says, "For this reason, a man shall leave his father and his mother, and be joined to his wife; and they shall become one flesh" (Genesis 2:24).

Before going further in this chapter, I have a question. Does God have a body? If God has a body, does being created in God's image mean we have a body like His? Jesus revealed that God is spirit (John 4:24; Luke 24:39). God is spirit means no physical body. If you read in the Bible what God can do as a spirit being, you will realize that a spirit can think, reason, exercise a will, see, hear, have emotions, and much more. When God created humans, He put His soul and spirit within our physical body. The soul and spirit can do things apart from a body. For example, what role of the spirit in our bodies can be seen in Romans 8:16? What do we learn about a spirit in Luke 8:52-55? Thus, we can say that being in God's image can refer to soul and spirit aspects of God within us that can operate apart from a physical body.

WHAT DOES IT MEAN THAT THE MAN AND THE WOMAN ARE CREATED IN GOD'S IMAGE?

If we look in a mirror, we see a reflection of ourselves. To be in God's image means we are a reflection of who God is. Since we are created to be imagers of God, it helps us to know what God is like. Thankfully, God gave us a standard and an example to follow. To show us what a human who bears the image of God looks like, God came to earth Himself, in the person of a man named Jesus. Jesus said, "He who has seen me, has seen the Father" (John 14:8-9). If we want to know what God is like, look at Jesus. Jesus is the perfect model of what it means to be truly human. He perfectly reflects, radiates, and represents the image and nature of God (Hebrews 1:2-3). That being the case, the more we are like Jesus, the more we will be like God. God's ultimate plan for those who love God is to be conformed to the image of His Son (Romans 8:28-29). We could say that to be in God's image is to look like Jesus in our character and in the way we think and live out our daily lives. Of course, we will not be able to do all Jesus does as the Savior of us all, but we can at least reflect God's seven spiritual characteristics mentioned in chapter four.

In the following seven statements, we shall focus on the seven characteristics of God that were listed in chapter four. Like Jesus, as a person who bears the image of God, I too embody these seven characteristics of Godlikeness. Following, I want to expand our thinking on the meaning of those seven characteristics. Understanding the triune nature of God is foundational in answering the question, "Who am I?"

WHO AM I?

One: I am a person created in the image of a God who cannot die; therefore, I am created to have His eternal life in me.

God is eternally self-sufficient. He depends on nothing outside of Himself for His existence. God is eternal life, along with the Son and Holy Spirit. I am not eternal like God. I am eternal only if God has created me to live forever, which He apparently did in his original creation. If God breathed His life/soul into man causing him to come to life (Genesis 2:7), is not God's forever kind of life the kind of life Adam received? Throughout the Bible there are statements by individuals testifying that eternal life was something they knew to be true. A wise person declared in Ecclesiastes 3:11 that God has put eternity in our hearts. Job testifies this belief when in the midst of his sufferings he said, "As for me, I know that my Redeemer lives, and at the last He will take His stand on the earth. Even after my skin is destroyed, yet from my flesh I shall see God; whom I myself shall behold, and whom my eyes will see and not another. My heart faints within me!" (Job 19:25-27). Read Jesus' statement in John 11:25-26, and Paul's statements in 1 Thessalonians 4:16-18 and 1 Corinthians 15:26. Is eternal life in spirit form only, or does our physical body also live forever by the power of God within us (Read 1 Corinthians 15:12-22 and Philippians 3:20-21) How important to you is knowing for sure that you have God's eternal life (Read 1 John 5:13)?

If God had not meant for human creatures to live forever, not only in spirit, but in body, why would He have warned Adam to avoid eating from a tree that would cause death (Genesis 2:16-17). Unfortunately, Adam did not heed God's warning, which brought death and the loss of God's eternal kind of life into our world (Romans 5:12). Fortunately, all is not lost, for God had already made a plan to enable us to overcome death. Christ is the way, and his resurrection from the dead certainly testifies to the truth of His words. He in us is our guarantee of eternal life (Romans 8:9-11). Later in this book there will be a detailed explanation of what the Bible says about how to get eternal life, and how to know that we have it.

WHO IS GOD? WHO AM I?

Two: I am a ruler under God, to rule and subdue the earth.

God is over all his created world (Psalm. 24:1). God created the earth to be inhabited (Isaiah 45:18). It is our home, for God has given the earth to the sons of men (Psalm 115:16). Being created in God's image means that together, the man and woman are given equal authority by God to rule and subdue the earth and all it contains. In Hebrew the word "subdue" is "Kabash," meaning "to control, to subdue, to have dominion over." Being created in God's image we have it in us to rule. Ruling and subduing are to be done under God and according to the will of God. What does God mean when He commands us to rule and subdue the earth? Ruling means we take responsibility as God's stewards to maintain what is good and right on the earth. We are to have control over ourselves, animals, and the environment. Following are five possible meanings or ways that we can rule and subdue. Perhaps you can think of more.

Five Ways to Rule and Subdue the Earth

First, God gives mankind work to do. God wants our work to be pleasurable, and of course, God wants our work to bring about positive production and to serve good purposes. For example, one way Adam ruled was to farm and maintain a garden so that it would be successful and beneficial to others by producing food for his and others' nourishment. Farmers today do the same, subduing the elements and producing food. I recently did business at a store and while visiting with one of the workers, the comment was made, "I don't know why I am here, accept to make money." I responded, "You are here for more than that. Your work is to help people. I needed your help today and am very appreciative you were here to help me."

Second, subduing recognizes that God put many wonderful resources in and on the earth. These resources are like treasures, some hidden so that we can have the joy of discovering, developing, and using them for our personal benefit and the benefit of mankind. What we discover allows us to make things like houses, musical instruments, cars, airplanes, medicines, electrical power, books for educational

WHO AM I?

purposes, and various media forms for communication. What we discover is more than producing needed products for ourselves and others; things we discover can be fun, entertaining, and may prompt enjoyable hobbies.

Third, we can subdue animals by training them for a variety of beneficial purposes, including helping us with our work, or to be comforting companions. Dangerous animals must be managed for our safety (Ezekiel 34:25). Animals often meet our needs for food or clothing, as well as being a source of income from which we make a living. On occasion the Bible promotes studying animals to learn lessons from them and to apply their ways to our lives. (Read for example Proverbs 6:6; Matthew 6:26)

Fourth, although God created a good world, God knows that there is such a thing as evil. He knows that If evil is allowed to gain access into the world, evil will destroy the good. God does not allow evil into His life (Psalm 5:4). Subduing means that man too must protect himself and the creation from evil and not allow wrongdoing to have its way. We must master natural inclinations, including evil thoughts, keeping them in check so evil and its dangers cannot overtake our lives and world. God warned humans about the potential for evil, and not to let it gain a foothold. (Read Genesis 2:16-17; 4:6-7; 2 Corinthians 10:5). Since mankind allowed evil to enter the world, subduing now includes having to overcome and put down destructive threats so good can survive (Romans 12:21). Enemies of our well-being can also include disease and sicknesses.

Fifth, because nature itself has become corrupted, things age and die. Since things tend to fall apart and quit working as they were designed, subduing means it is necessary to keep the world in repair. Like God, we must supply whatever energy is needed to keep things working properly. The authority given us to subdue all things has not been taken away due to the invasion of evil. Subduing has now been made difficult and sometimes seemingly impossible. Sadly, although we are created in God's image, we often fail to take care to protect ourselves and our world from further corruption, including keeping our earth clean and looking beautiful.

WHO IS GOD? WHO AM I?

We do these things today, don't we? Can you think of other ways mankind has ruled over and subdued the earth? Doing science is a good discipline to learn about the world and how it works. Many scientific discoveries lead to ways we can best subdue, use, and take care of the world around us.

Example: How Israel's Kings are to Rule

This exercise is about God's law for the kings who are to rule over God's people. Again, the purpose of these exercises is to slow down and think about "Who is God?." and "Who am I?" Subduing the earth is all about using our authority for good and to achieve God's purposes. Although we are not kings, this exercise can apply to each of us in areas of authority where we are responsible for the well-being of others. Having authority for the well-being of others can include our role as parents, managers in our jobs, school-teachers, college professors, politicians, leaders of organizations such as boy scouts, girl scouts, sports teams, community projects, and so on.

Read Deuteronomy 17:14-20. Name all the things the king is to do and not do? Read also Psalm 33:16-17; 1 Kings 11:1-6; Proverbs 3:13-15. After reading these scriptures, can you answer why the king was not to focus on horses, multiple wives, or wealth? Why would paying daily attention to God's word make the king a good and better leader? If God chooses the king, why does He want the citizens to have a role in choosing their ruler? What do you think God is concerned about in giving these rules? What positions of authority do you have? Is there anything here that would be good to apply to your position? Who is God? How does God want me to rule over people and things under my care? Who am I? How can I best rule?

Three: I am a relational being.

God is a relational being. He loves, communicates, reasons, wills to act, and has divine feelings (read Jeremiah 8:18-22). Like God, I communicate and interact with the world around me. God's trinitarian relationship is love. The Son loves the Father and the Father loves the

WHO AM I?

Son (John 14:31; 17.24). 1 John 4:8 says, "The one who does not love does not know God, for God is love." The Bible says much about love. "We love because He first loved us" (1 John 4:19). Jesus said I am to love others as God has loved me (John 15:12). He also said that people will know we are followers of Him by how we love one another (John 13:35). A good model of God's love is the person of Jesus who came to earth to show us what God is like. Jesus teaches us things that are involved in loving, such as doing good (Acts 10:38), rightly judging people (Matthew 7:1-5; John 7:24; Romans 2:1-6), and forgiving (Matthew 6:14-15). A good definition to see how well we are doing at loving is 1 Corinthians 13:4-8. Since we now live in an evil world, and evil ways live in us, to love as God loves is a difficult thing to do. Nevertheless, those who are a new creation in Christ (2 Corinthians 5:17) are being restored to love. God's love is not as most humans of this world define it, but as God originally meant it to be. Our love is to be like the love practiced between the three beings in God's triune nature.

Example: How we can grow in God's love.

Because we are created in God's image, we all have within us a sense that we need to love and be loved. Unfortunately, we often fail at loving ourselves, God, and others. God says love never fails, yet, people who fall in love, can also fall out of love. The world is full of hate and anger, yet somehow, we know that what the world wants and needs is love. The scriptures about love are true. God created us to love. It is God's greatest commandment (Matthew 22:36-39). God wants us to be like Him (Matthew 5:48). Though we can't be perfect, we can have God's kind of love as our goal. How then can we get better at it?

Read and think about how practicing Romans 8:5-13 can help us. In this passage, what two things are at odds with each other? List all that is said about the flesh, and things of the flesh. List all that is said about the Spirit, and things of the Spirit. In the Old Testament, God's people were not living as He wanted them to live. According to Ezekiel 11:19-20 and 36:26-27, what did God promise to do to help them live His way? How did God fulfill His promise according to Romans 8:9-

WHO IS GOD? WHO AM I?

11? If Christ is in you, pause to accept what is true about you in Romans 8:1-4, and thank Him. Rather than put yourself down each time you fail in loving someone as God would want, ask Him to show you how to use your failure as a steppingstone to improve. Growing in love is a spiritual work in progress. Keep focusing on becoming who God created you to be. Slow down and think: What is God's love like? How am I seeking to do it better? Read again 1 Corinthians 13:4-7.

Four: I am an interdependent being.

Consider the following four words and what they mean. (1) "Interdependent" means we depend on each other for our well-being. Members of the triune God give to each other and receive from each other. Because I am created in God's image, I receive what you have to give me and you receive what I have to give you. (2) "Dependent" means that as humans we rely on something or someone outside of ourselves for what we need. That is true. We do need others to help us. But to be one sided, always taking from others and never giving, would not result in ours or others total well-being. God does not rely on anything outside of Himself for His well-being. He is self-sufficient. All three persons in God's being operate by giving and receiving. (3) "Independent" means humans are relying on themselves for what they need. Independent can mean I don't need you. I can do it myself. Such is impossible, for we all need others. God is not independent since He relies on the other persons within Himself to make Him complete. (4) "Codependency" is a word humans use when they are trapped in a dysfunctional relationship that is emotionally and behaviorally unhealthy for the persons involved. If we are overly dependent, or independent, or codependent, we get out of balance and life does not work as it ought. God's inter-relationships between the three persons are in perfect harmony and they work together to accomplish what is good. God, as a triunity, is a diverse being with perfect unity. Following are good illustrations of "unity in diversity", showing how interdependence is what makes unity possible.

One good illustration of unity in diversity and interdependence is the Bible's description of the human body. God created our body to

WHO AM I?

work like His own diverse, yet interdependent nature (1 Corinthians 12:12-26). I am an interdependent being because my body is one body with many parts, all differing from the others. I have eyes, a heart, feet, hands, muscles, blood vessels, a brain, nerves, a mouth (which can get me into trouble), and many other parts. Although I am one body, all the parts work together for the body's good and well-being. For example, if I cut myself and am bleeding, my nerves alert me to pain, my eyes see what's happening, my brain tells my feet to go get a bandage, my muscles help me get there, and my hands wash the injury and apply the band aid. Each part, has a task to perform and they don't rebel, but willingly do what's needed. Giving and receiving is natural. Interdependence is how God created us to be.

Another illustration of unity in diversity and interdependence is communities in society. Each person contributes something for the good of the community. In this way the community can be unified, have its needs or wants met, and enjoy peace and harmony. We, as part of a community, give what we have to help others, and we are all helped when we receive what they give to us. The beauty of interdependency is working together to achieve the community goals. For example, the community I lived in wanted an indoor hockey arena. Individuals gave what they could to make it happen and others received what was given to complete the project. It would not have been done without each other. The community also helps each other out when members suffer misfortune, perhaps bad health or a sudden tragedy. How the church community is supposed to work as a body is also a good illustration of unity in diversity and interdependence (Read Ephesians 4:7-16). Interdependence is how unity in diversity is achieved.

A third illustration of unity in diversity and interdependence is also the way God's creation of the whole world works. Nature is made in the image of God, for it consists of many parts, giving and receiving, so that all of nature is unified and complete as its parts work together.

The Bible presents us with this question, "What do you have that you did not receive" (1 Corinthians 4:7)? That being true, as interdependent beings, there is no room for boasting or feeling superior to anyone. Realizing who we are, each of us will tend to be grateful, offering thanks to everyone for what he or she has given us. We will

WHO IS GOD? WHO AM I?

also be thankful for what God's created world gives us, and we will give back to it by taking care of it.

Five: I am part of a hierarchy.

In the following paragraphs I discuss a controversial topic concerning men and women. Please know before you read this that I am simply seeking to describe a human problem and I'm asking if God's triune nature contributes to a solution. God created us in his image as male and female. He created "us" to be one, for He also is an "us" and is one. In God's triunity, there is headship and submission. There is an order of authority, a head in charge, and members of the triune God willingly choosing to submit to each other in maintaining that oneness. Just as hierarchy exists in God's person, if we are made in his image, would we not expect hierarchy to exist in human relationships? We all live in a world of God's making that involves someone in authority and others submitting to that authority. Being under governmental authority is one example (Read Romans 13:1-2).

The Bible uses the word "head" for someone in charge and to whom others submit. For example, "Christ is the head of every man, and man is the head of a woman, and God is the head of Christ" (1 Corinthians 11:3). The meaning of the word "head" has caused much controversy in today's modern culture, primarily over issues regarding men and women. For example, to say that man is the head of woman is said to be demeaning to women. It is bad to imply that men are superior to women, therefore there is a battle to establish the equality of men and women. Both sides argue about the word "head." Does "head" mean "authority over," or does "head" mean "the source of"? For example, does "head" mean God is the source of Jesus, or man is the source of woman? One side, labeled "Traditionalist" or "Complementarianism," argues that the man, as head of the woman, is responsible to lead, for example, as husband in the home. Women are expected to submit to that leadership. The other side, labeled, "Egalitarianism", argues that men and women need to be submissive to one another as equals. After all, the Bible does say that "there is neither male nor female; for you are all one in Christ Jesus" (Galatians 3:28).

WHO AM I?

Women are often encouraged to affirm their equality and not give in to any hierarchical relationship in marriage. We are equal. So are the members of God's triune being. But that does not eliminate hierarchy in an equal-person relationship by excluding headship of one over another. The problem often actually stems from abuses of headship.

If we reject authority because we have been abused by someone's authority, our tendency will be to reject authority and make ourselves our own authority. Understandably so, because out of fear or hatred of further abuse, we strive to protect ourselves from those abusers. Abuse from authorities will give us cause not to trust any authority. True, we must not allow those abuses to continue, but we must also know there is authority in the world that we need and ought to trust. God has ordained properly executed authority for our wellbeing (Roman 13:1-7). Therefore, we need to throw off the bad, but yield to the good.

The modern-day church also struggles with this issue of headship. Bible scholars have contested Biblical statements that imply a hierarchy among the persons within the triune nature of God (John 5:30; 6:38; 14:28; 15:10). One thought they promote is this: If the Father is the authority over the Son, then the Father and the Son are not equally God. But since the Father and Son are equally God, hierarchy only applies when the Son became a man and was made lesser than God. Jesus then became subject to the Father's will. To take the other side, let's suppose that from all eternity past, there is hierarchy among the persons of the triune God. When we study the hierarchical relationship between the persons of the triune God, we find that there is love between them, not abuse, nor any feelings of one being less than another. They are all equally God, and yet, there is no problem of one being willingly submissive to the other. Apparently, all members of God's triunity are happy with the arrangement and are in complete harmony with one another. If we, as men and women, are created in the image of God, and if there is not a problem with headship in the triunity, why is there a problem with headship between men and women in today's world? Could it be that the problem between men and women exists because we do not understand how hierarchy works in the triunity. Or could the problem be that men abuse what it means to be "head," and all of us abuse what it means to be submissive? Instead of

WHO IS GOD? WHO AM I?

trying to understand what it means to be created in God's image as men and women, we take sides and try to prove one side over the other by arguments like the differences over the meaning of the word "head." If the meaning of the word "head" intrigues or confuses you, you might find it rewarding to read an extensive study of the word by Wayne Grudem.[11]

I have noticed what often happens when persons take one side of any issue over another. Usually, I find there is truth on both sides. But I also discover there is something that is not right on both sides. What often happens is that, when people see or experience what is not right, they react by adopting an opposing side. But in doing this, without looking deeper at both sides, (thinking they've thoroughly checked it out), they create division between people. The division is created by the self-justified attitude "I'm right and they are wrong." When this happens two very important things may be lost. (1) By thinking my view is the right one, I cannot read the Bible correctly because I will take verses that seem not to fit my view and make them, so they agree with me. (2) By rejecting persons who are not agreeing with me, or who are exhibiting negative attitudes toward me, there is a loss of love and care for them. It's easy to find and care for people who agree with us, and dismiss persons who do not.

I was reading a book by Dr. Larry Crabb. He told of a time when God said something to him through a friend's comment. It changed his thinking. Dr. Crabb asked his respected friend, "Why is it, do you suppose, that people have such a hard time getting along with each other?" Without hesitation his friend answered, "Well, the whole thing comes down to selfishness, doesn't it. Isn't it interesting how people complicate it all so much? I suppose we don't like seeing ourselves as we really are." [12] Dr. Crabb had been thinking about the issue of complementarianism versus egalitarianism. It caused him to realize that

---

[11] Wayne Grudem, "Does Kephalyn (Head) mean 'Source' or 'Authority over' in Greek Literature?" A Survey of 2,336 Examples" (Trinity Journal ns. 6.1, Spring 1985, pgs. 38-59.

[12] Dr. Larry Crabb, "Men and Women: Enjoying the Difference" (Zondervan Publishing House, Grand Rapids, MI, 1991), p. 86.

WHO AM I?

the issue would not be resolved by choosing one side over the other, based on how each side perceives scripture. He goes on to relate in his book that both sides are guilty of self-centeredness, perhaps trying to control a situation due to some fear, and until that issue is faced and dealt with, it won't do any good to keep arguing about which view is right. He recognizes that understanding God's three-in-one nature is key to becoming who God made us to be as men and women. Unlike self-centered human relationships, God is a hierarchical being consisting of three persons, and God has no problem with authority and submission. There is no problem with one person feeling inferior to the other. There is no problem with one person dominating the other, nor committing verbal or any other kind of abuse. There is no problem with self-centeredness because each member of God's triune nature is devoted to giving unreservedly to the well-being of the whole. Apparently, there is something in our knowledge of God's nature, the nature that He has put into us, that is missing in our consideration of how to live our lives. If we model our lifestyle after God's image in us, and become other-centered rather than self-centered, we would go a long way to resolving our differences. Are we lacking God's kind of love when we claim we are right, and they are wrong and that we have the Bible on our side to prove it?

Through my own misbehaviors and errant attitudes in causing strife, I have been learning, and am still learning, the importance of giving grace to those who disagree with me. Giving God's grace means that instead of arguing and defending my own views, I seek to understand the other person and what makes them take the views they do. The best way to understand another is to listen to them, and to be able to ask questions that help them express why they believe what they do. The bottom line is to see what motivates them. Of course, I must examine my own heart first to discover the truth of why I believe as I do. God looks past the outer appearance of things and looks at our heart. Often, we do not even know who we ourselves are unless God points it out to us, for He knows all things and sees what we cannot see or are unwilling to see (Proverbs 21:2; 1 Samuel 16:7; Luke 16:15). Even if we do disagree with others, there are ways to preserve unity in the midst of diversity so that the prayer of Jesus can be answered (John 17:20-

21). The Bible shows us ways to do this, for example through practicing the teachings of Romans 14, or through understanding the attitude of the apostle Paul when people were against him (1 Corinthians 4:1-5). Ultimately, unity is learned by considering the nature of the triune God. God is a God who submits through self-sacrifice to each other within Himself so that the will of God is accomplished (Philippians 2:3-11; Ephesians 5:21; Mark 10:44-45). We are all called to practice the will of God (Matthew 7:21; 1 Peter 4:1-2; 1 John 2:17) Someone defined the will of God as "doing the right thing, for the right reason, at the right time."

Six: I am a free-will person.

Free will has to do with having the right and responsibility to choose among various options. God plans and makes choices of what He will do or not do (for example, Exodus 32:9-14; Jeremiah 26:12-13; Amos 7:1-6; Jonah 3:10). Thus, He created us to have free will. We can even change our mind and will if there is a change in circumstances. The world tries to convince us that we do not have free will. The fatalist believes "What will be will be. We might as well accept it; we can't change what happens." Some scientists say, "Everything that happens to us is caused by the brain or by a chain of events that came before us. Our choices are determined by those causes, not by free will." Some theologians strongly emphasize that God is sovereign; He does not change (for example, 1 Samuel 15:24-29), and nothing happens apart from His control. This view also challenges our notion that we have free will. These kinds of beliefs, "whatever will be will be", "everything has a cause outside of us" (which is partly true), or "God determines everything," make it easy to give in to feelings like "Why should I try to make a difference in the world, everything is already set."

The conclusion that we have no free will does not fit with what we read in the Bible, nor does it agree with what we experience. When we read the Bible, we see that God gives persons the freedom to choose. We are aware of lots of choices that we make every day. The Bible and our own experiences convince us that we have free will. In the Bible, it

WHO AM I?

is true, we do see that God is a sovereign God who determines what happens in people's lives. This is another of those mysterious issues with two sides that are hard to reconcile. How can God be sovereign if He allows free will, and how can we have free will if God is sovereign? I cannot always figure things out, but I do believe that this is one of those areas where the truth lies simultaneously at both ends. If I choose one end over the other, I will run into problems that in some way will not allow me to be able to live as God intended. One problem that I have observed is that people with an over emphasis on God's sovereignty often lack love. And persons with an over emphasis on free will can lack a firm trust in God. Believing both things, even if we do not understand how it works, at least keeps our lives in balance so that we can do both. We can trust God's sovereignty and make a difference through the choices we make. God made us like Himself, to be change agents. In fact, we often work with God to help change things in our world for the good (1 Corinthians 3:9). Also, God's ultimate determined plan for this world will happen as He has planned (Isaiah 14:21-27).

Seven: I am a moral being.

Like God, who distinguishes between good and evil, I have a moral compass inside of me that says there is such a thing as right and wrong, good and evil. God teaches us His morals by giving us laws that detail right from wrong, for example, His Ten Commandments (Exodus 20:1-17; Deuteronomy 5:1-33). He urges His people to do them so they can experience a good life, so that all might be well with them (Deuteronomy 5:32-33). However, because we fall far short and fail to live out God's laws, we must face the wrath and judgment of God. Fortunately for us, the loving mercy of the three persons of God, all doing their part, provides the answer to our problem. That answer involves God the Father sending His Son to be the Savior of the world (1 John 4:14). It involves Jesus Christ offering up His life to rescue us from this present evil world (Galatians 1:3-4). It involves the Holy Spirit coming to live within us (Romans 8:11), changing our stubborn

WHO IS GOD? WHO AM I?

heart into a willing heart (Ezekiel 36:26-27), and helping us to live a life that is morally honoring and pleasing to God (Galatians 5:16-23).

PSALM 25: DEEPENING OUR RELATIONSHIP WITH GOD

Often, the problems we have in life are caused by other people. This is a good Psalm to go to if you have people against you. In the last days, the Bible says God's people, Christians and Jews, will have lots of people against them (Matthew 24:9-13, 21-22). We will live in a world that is largely ungodly. To survive, we will need a deeper relationship with God. This Psalm can be divided into five sections. The goal is to understand the Psalmist's relationship with God and apply it to oneself. Answer the following questions for each section to discover what the Psalmist's relationship with God is like.

The five sections are: 25:1-3, 4-7, 8-11, 12-15, and 16-22. The questions for each section are:

1. What does the Psalm writer say about God? (Who is God?)
2. What does the Psalm writer say about himself?[13] (Who am I?)
3. What does the Psalmist believe about God?
4. What does the writer see are his responsibilities in the relationship?

At the end of the sections, ask yourself: What would I like my relationship with God to be like? Tell God.

---

[13] In Psalm 25:1-3 the word "ashamed" is from the Hebrew word "bosh", בוש and it is used 3 times. What does ashamed mean? It can mean disappointed in oneself due to sin or failure, feeling guilty, feeling I'm no good, a feeling of losing one's honor or reputation in a community, embarrassment, a fearful feeling of being humiliated, etc. It could be a legitimate feeling because you really did do something wrong, or it could be based on a lie being told about you and is no fault of your own. In a Biblical verse or passage, the context needs to be understood to determine the correct feeling that is meant.

WHO AM I?
A WORD ABOUT OUR RELATIONSHIP WITH GOD

At one end of our relationship is what God does for me, and at the other end is what I do for God. If I emphasize one end over the other, the relationship is out of kilter. Does life revolve around me and does God exist primarily for me? Am I constantly asking God for what I need or want? Do I expect Him to be on call whenever I need Him? Our relationship with God will be one-sided when it's all about me. On the other end, God doesn't only exist for me, but I exist for Him, (see Isaiah 43:6-7). I glorify God when I honor Him by being like Him. I would have nothing without His love, mercy, and forgiveness. It is true that in the "Lord's Prayer" (Matthew 6:9-13), Jesus taught us to ask God the Father for what we need. But notice that the prayer begins by addressing "Our Father." We focus on the presence of our Father.[14] Then we pray "hallowed be your name" (Matthew 6:9). What are we asking God to do? We are asking God to guide us in paths of righteousness for His name's sake (Psalm 23:4). We are asking that God would glorify His name by making it holy to people around us. How does He do that? Being created in His image means we are imagers of Godlikeness to those around us in order to mirror what God is like to others. We can easily profane His name by failing to look like Him and be like Him; by failing to live the way He designed us to live. We profane God's name when we disobey His righteous ways (Jeremiah 34:12-17; Ezekiel 20:8-17). Jesus said that we are to be the light of the world, so men may see our good works and glorify our Father who is in heaven (Matthew 5:14-16). We can choose to often begin our prayer each day with these words, "Father, hallowed be your name in me today."

One of the Ten Commandments says, "Do not take the name of the Lord in vain" (Exodus 20:7). When I was growing up I was taught not to use His name as a swear word. But it means much more than that. It

---

[14] Each time you start a prayer with "Our Father", you could read or remember one or more of these verses and thank Him for what He's done for you. Deut. 32:4-6, 18; Isa. 64:8; 9:6-7; Matt. 6:25-26; 5:14-16; John 3:1-3; 15:1-2; 2 Corinthians 1:3-4; James 1:17-18; 1 Peter 1:3-5.

means do not take on His name and then live differently than He designed you to live. Do not take His name in vain means do not say you follow Him and He is your God and then fail to willingly and lovingly bring your life to be in line with Jesus' teachings (John 14:15). Do not call Jesus Lord and then deny Him by doing things that are wrong. For example, stealing would cause me to profane the name of my God (Proverbs 30:8-9). In our relationship with God we are to balance asking God for something with giving what God wants from us. Another way to put it: (1) God gives to me (Romans 8:32; Matthew 7:11) to meet my needs, and (2) I give to God by being the person God has created me to be. (1 Corinthians 10:31; Luke 9:23-24) By imaging Him, I am serving His purposes for me and glorifying Him. This is not always easy due to sin. Praying often for God's help can move us in the right direction and so can being thankful for all things (1 Thessalonians 5:18). "Lord, keep me in true humility and away from self-centered pride. Amen" (James 4:6).

WHY WOULD GOD CREATE US TO BE LIKE HIM?

This question came to me and so I gave it some thought. The first thing I thought was that it would only be natural for God to make us like Himself. As His children, we are like who God is. Let's think for a moment what it means to be creators of our own children. As parents, when we produce a child, that child carries our DNA. Naturally, that child is in many ways like who we are. People will even comment how the child looks like us. "There can be no mistake," they say, "who that child belongs to." Who we are as parents naturally becomes a part of who our children are and who they become. When we train our children to grow up to be mature adults, we want them to think and act like us, at least the good parts of us. We want them to live by the morals we pass on to them, even to have faith in God if that is something we highly value. In a very real way, our children represent us and what we stand for, and if we have a good relationship with them and they love us, they will want to please us and make us proud of them. If they do good, we may even boast with comments like, "that's my daughter," or "that's my son." They grow up watching us, and they see what we are like and

WHO AM I?

how we do things, and they copy us. Our example teaches them how to live. Admittedly, as humans, we are not all exactly the same, but we do take on similar characteristics of the ones who brought us into the world. We can feel embarrassed if our offspring does something bad that disappoints us, something we would not do. We want them to obey us. Why? Because we think it's going to result in a good life if they do. There may also be an ulterior motive because the actions of our children reflect on us. We have a reputation we try to uphold, and we don't want their actions to give us a bad name. As children, we come to realize that we don't exist just for ourselves. We carry on the good name and honor of our parents and family. I remember a comment our daughter once made to our son. He was misbehaving and she said to him, "Our family doesn't do that." To me, these are reasons God creates us in His image. God creates us to be like Him because He knows that there is no better life outside of the one He gives to us, and He wants us to have the best life we can have. And isn't that what we want for our kids? Especially, if we grew up having a bad or hard life, we want our children to have it better than we did. We may even try and help that to happen. Admittedly, although parents may try to do the best they can at raising their children, any child can exercise their God-given free will and go another way. That happens to God all the time. God's children also choose to rebel. Why would God create us to be like Him? It's who He is; it's natural for Him to make us imagers, that is, reflectors of who He is. As Jesus, the Son of God said, "He who has seen me has seen the Father" (John 14:9). The fully human Jesus was a perfect image of who His Father is. As our heavenly Father, we also were designed to look like the God who made us. Speaking of unifying factors, living the above seven attributes of God are essential in unifying a divided world. But as you could tell by reading the above descriptions of these seven traits of God, God's image in us has been spoiled. All of us have fallen short of being like God created us to be. Why? What happened? What went wrong? That is the subject of the next chapter.

Chapter 6

BAD NEWS — WHAT WENT WRONG

REVIEW OF THE LAST CHAPTER

In the last chapter we applied the inner relationships of the "three-persons in one God" to ourselves. To be created in God's image is to be representatives of what God is like. We considered that the following characteristics of God are in us and are thus a basic part of who we are. Let's review them again:

> If God is an eternal being, I am created to be an eternal being, though not self-existent as is God.
>
> If God rules and cares for His creation, as a good steward, I am created to rule and care for the creation.
>
> If God is a relational being, I am created to communicate with others, to know others and to be known.
>
> If God is an interdependent being, I am created to give to others and receive from others.
>
> If God is hierarchical in structure, I am created to be part of a lifestyle involving authority and submission.
>
> If God is a free-will being, I am created to be a free-will being.
>
> If God is a moral being, I am created to be a virtuous, good, and honest person, free of all evil.

After God created the world and all that is in it, He declared that all was good. For the man and his wife there was no evil to destroy what was good. The natural world they lived in was peaceful and safe. They had everything they needed to sustain their lives. As man and wife they had a harmonious relationship. All things worked well together. But then something happened to change things for the worse. Although we were made to be good like God, it has become clear that we humans

WHO IS GOD? WHO AM I?

are no longer good like God. What happened? What went wrong? Who am I? We shall explore the answer to that question in this chapter.

THE BAD NEWS

Even though people are no longer like God made them to be, there is still something of God's goodness in us and in the world. However, no one is good like God is good (Mark 10:18). We are corrupted. Love is tainted by hate, patience is tainted with impatience, peace is tainted by war, caring for one another is tainted by abuses, right thinking and wisdom is tainted by errors in judgment, truth is tainted by lies, greediness for personal wealth and gain overcomes genuine concern for the needs of others. Effective communication and loving each other is destroyed by broken and dysfunctional relationships filled with dishonesty, anger, division, and pain. Instead of being interdependent, we are often overly dependent or pridefully independent. Looking out for our own interests replaces submitting to God's good will. Instead of using our free will for good, we have become prisoners to the evils that enslave and surround us.

Nature has also been corrupted (Romans 8:20-21). There are evils such as storms, diseases, extreme temperatures, floods, and birth defects. Instead of enjoying an abundant life, all living things die. Instead of subduing the earth for good purposes, we often misuse and abuse it for our own purposes. This is not how nature, including humans, was originally created. Nature and life are now a long way from what they were created to be. We are not now good imagers of God able to live the good life He made for us.

HOW EVIL ENTERED OUR WORLD - WHAT WENT WRONG?

To learn how things went wrong, here is an exercise for you to do that will cover Genesis 3:1-24. Time to slow down again and think about some scriptures. The following questions, whether or not we get all the answers right, will stimulate our thinking as we continue to learn more about "who is God" and "who am I." How did evil come into the world, and how is it affecting all of mankind today? As you attempt to

BAD NEWS — WHAT WENT WRONG

answer these questions, it might prove helpful to discuss them with others.

Read Genesis 3:1-13.

1. Name the persons involved in these verses. How do we know God gave Adam and Eve a free will? Remember, free will is to be able to choose amidst options. What were the options?

2. According to 3:1, what was said about the serpent? Does 2 Corinthians 11:3; Revelation 12:9; 20:2 add anything to our knowledge about the serpent? Who do you think the serpent was? What did Jesus say about the devil in John 8:44? Do you believe, like Jesus, that there is a devil? Why or why not?

3. What does the deceiver want the woman to believe about God and herself? How does Satan deceive the woman and cause her to have doubts? What does the woman doubt?

4. Why do you think the woman listens to the serpent and gives in to the devil's lies? Can you think of any reasons why the serpent's words in 3:5 would be appealing to the woman?

5. Do you think Adam was present and heard Satan's conversation with Eve? —consider Genesis 3:6.

<u>Comments concerning question 5</u>: 1 Timothy 2:13-14 says, "For it was Adam who was first created, then Eve. And it was not Adam who was deceived, but the woman being deceived, fell into transgression." You may have heard comments that it was the woman's fault that sin entered the world. But if Adam was with her during the temptation, and he was not deceived, should he not have spoken up and helped his wife resist the temptation. He knew God's word to them was to not eat of that tree.

WHO IS GOD? WHO AM I?

But once Eve yielded to temptation and ate of the tree, if he knew better, why would Adam eat of it? Not being deceived, when he ate from the tree, he knew for a fact it was wrong, therefore he went against God by disobeying God's word. Thus, the man was more responsible for the fall into sin than the woman because he deliberately disobeyed God. Whether Adam was with the woman during the temptation, or not, people may wonder, "Why would he take from Eve and eat what was forbidden if he knew it was wrong?" Here is an answer some give. Of course, we are free to disagree and free to consider no answer or a better answer. From what Genesis 2:22-24 says, Adam felt it was not good to be alone. He knew that God brought Eve to him to be his wife and companion. God said they were to become one flesh. Jesus interpreted this in Mark 10 when he commented, "What therefore God has joined together, let no man separate." Did not God bring them together to be one? Was Adam fearful for what might happen to his wife? Did Adam, still a person without sin, have a sense of God's love, even for those who are sinners? What a position to be in, to be faced with this temptation and to love someone dear to him, but to go against God in order to join with her. He would be committing a conscious act of sin against God to put himself and his wife ahead of God's warning. Somehow, he chose to go against God. And then, as a sinner, out of fear, instead of taking responsibility for letting sin into his life and into the world, as a self-justification before God, he blamed his wife for giving it to him. By eating of the tree of good and evil, Adam and his wife now both knew the devastating evil of going against God. The same is true today, we all have within ourselves an experiential knowledge of good and evil. Unfortunately, we too have made our choices to go against God and the evil cannot be undone. Thankfully, what is impossible for man, is possible with God (Luke 18:26-27). Although we cannot save ourselves, God can by sending His Son (Read Romans 5:12-21; Ephesians 2:1-10).

6. In Genesis 3:7, What was the immediate consequence of their wrongdoing? How did their relationship with God change?

BAD NEWS — WHAT WENT WRONG

7. When they ate from the tree they did not physically die immediately. Why do you think not? What does spiritual death mean? (see Ephesians 2:1-3; John 3:36) When do you think they died spiritually?

8. According to 3:8, what did they do when God came for a visit? How did the man and woman know God was there? Why would they know who it was? How do we hide from God today?

9. According to 3:9-11, how did God approach the man and woman when they were hiding? Do you think there was any significance in the fact that God addresses the man first? What questions did God ask? Why does God ask them, and what affect would these questions have on Adam and Eve?

10. What was the name of the tree from which Adam and Eve ate (2:17)? What did Adam and Eve know about good and evil before they ate from the tree? (2:16-17; 3:1-3) What did they know after they ate? (3:22) Do you think good and evil continue to exist in today's world? Why or why not?

11. What do you think was the sin of the man and woman? What did they fail to do and why? What was the wrong Adam did in this situation? Is God mean or egotistical for wanting people to trust Him and obey Him? Why or why not?

<u>Comments concerning questions from 11 above:</u> God knew that evil is potentially destructive and causes a ruination of life. God placed in front of the man and woman a tree of the knowledge of good and evil. All other trees were good, but this one was to be avoided. God told the man and woman not to partake of it. The man and woman do not have to partake of evil to know there is such a thing as evil. They did not

have to try it to know if it was bad or not. God told them. They needed to trust God's word on that. God told Adam that he was not to eat from this tree. God had a good reason for saying this for He knew that if they did not do as He said, they would die. They were like God in that God knows about good and evil, but unlike God in that God never gives in to evil. God does not let evil become a part of who He is. To what extent do you believe man's free will has been damaged? Why do you think God gives us the freedom to choose? (Consider Deuteronomy 8:2-3 and Genesis 22:1-2, 12) Does it reveal where our heart is, if with God or not?

COMPARING THE MAN ADAM AND THE MAN JESUS (SEE ROMANS 5:14; 1 CORINTHIANS 15:45-49)

Read Matthew 4:1-10. The man, Jesus, can be compared to the man, Adam. Both were sinless when the devil came along to try to get them to do wrong. Both knew about good and evil, but not by experiencing it. Both Adam and Jesus knew: "Do this, but don't do that"; "Eat the fruit from any tree, but not from that tree or it will ruin your life." What does the devil say to try and get Jesus to doubt God? Jesus had been fasting 40 days and was hungry. "If you are the Son of God", says the devil, "Command that these stones become bread." The tempter must have known that the first man and woman had a hunger to satisfy something within them. Jesus felt the need to satisfy a hunger within him, so the devil appeals to the hunger Jesus was experiencing. If Jesus is really God's Son, and wants to be like God, he should make his own food. How does Jesus respond? Immediately, the word of God comes to Jesus' mind and he quotes God's word to the devil. "Man shall not live on bread alone, but on every word that proceeds out of the mouth of God" (Deuteronomy 8:3). Jesus listened and obeyed what God said. The devil tries again. Knowing that Jesus believes the word of God in the Bible, the devil quotes the word of God that says "if you throw yourself down, God will command His angels to save you" (Psalm 91:11-12). The devil tells Jesus to jump off a high place, "God will save you; you won't die." The devil did the same with the man and woman when he told them they could eat of the tree, and they would

BAD NEWS — WHAT WENT WRONG

not die. Jesus responded, "You shall not put the Lord your God to the test (Deuteronomy 6:16). The devil tried one more time. He showed Jesus all the kingdoms of the world and their glory. He said that if Jesus would fall down and worship him, he would give these to Jesus. From God's word, Jesus knew that one day he would be able to ask God for the world and God would give it to him (Psalm 2:7-8). Satan tempted him by offering the world to him now, so he would not have to wait. Jesus told Satan to leave and gave him these words of God, "You shall worship the Lord your God, and serve Him only" (Deuteronomy 10:20). Jesus did what Adam and Eve did not do. Both Jesus and Adam had God's word on what God told them to do. Jesus heard what Satan was telling him to do and knowing that it was not what God's word said to do, Jesus refused to let evil enter his life. Jesus knew about good and evil, and he refused to let the devil get him to take matters into his own hands. Instead, Jesus trusted and obeyed God.

WHO IS MAN?

In a way, the devil told Adam and the Eve the truth but mixed it with a lie. Yes, they would be like God, knowing good and evil, but they would know good and evil differently than God knew it. They would know evil by experiencing it, and by experiencing it, they would know what God knew; that evil ruins life just as He said it would. How did it ruin their lives? They immediately felt ashamed, they knew they were no longer like God created them to be. They lost their harmonious fellowship with God. Knowing they were guilty of wrong-doing, they became afraid to face God. They hid from God and were unwilling to take responsibility for their wrongs. Instead, they justified their behavior by blaming others for what happened. Most of all, they lost God's kind of life. They were put out of the garden so they could not eat from the tree of life. They did not physically die immediately, but they did die spiritually in that they knew they were now separated from God, no longer one with Him in love and in purpose. Although God still loved them, they must now be given a way to regain their knowledge of God's love and be restored to their oneness with God. They had become self-conscious, self-centered, and self-protective.

WHO IS GOD? WHO AM I?

Their spirits were no longer in tune with God's Spirit. They were no longer good representatives of the image of God. By their sin, they profaned God's image. Although remnants of His likeness still existed in them, they lost their perfect God likeness. They knew both good and evil. They knew they should be good like God, and they knew that evil was not good. But now, it became a losing battle to do good and overcome the harms of evil, both within them, and in the world around them. Now, they were in a position that they could not undo what they had done. This is the problem we all have today. Our conscience knows better (if it is working properly), but we choose to do wrong, we experience evil, and it has become embedded within us (see Romans 7:18-24). Wrongdoing has become a huge part of each of our lives and of the world we live in. It has changed and damaged our relationship with God and with each other. Mankind's whole environment was also corrupted (Romans 8:20-21).

GOD'S PUNISHMENT

Read Genesis 3:14-24. God punishes Satan, the woman, and the man. Questions to think about.

1. How does God punish Satan? (3:14-15) As a part of Satan's punishment, what does God prophesy?

2. How does God punish the woman? (3:16)

3. How does God punish Adam? (3:17-24)

Notice that even with God's right to judge and destroy evil, He gives grace by not allowing death to come immediately. What hope do you see God giving to the guilty that all may not be lost?

HOW BAD CAN EVIL BECOME?

Read Genesis 4:1-16.

BAD NEWS — WHAT WENT WRONG

1. Adam and his family have been banned from the garden of Eden and from the tree of life. Yet, in spite of their restrictions, there seems to be an ongoing connection between the Lord and the members of Adam's family. What do we observe that the relationship is like between the Lord and the persons named? Is there anything positive along with the negative?

2. With whom was Cain angry and why was his face gloomy? (4:3-5)

3. What does the Lord say to Cain about his feelings? (4:6-7) What does the Lord want Cain to realize? What is the Lord saying about Cain's responsibilities? What does this say about man's free will?

4. What was Cain's response to God's warnings? (4:8)

5. What did the Lord ask Cain after Cain killed his brother? (4:9) God knows what Cain did. Why do you think the Lord asks him this question?

6. What is Cain's answer to God? (4:9) Why do you think Cain lies? What does this say about Cain's heart?

7. What is the Lord's next response? Why ask this question and what evidence does God present to let Cain know he is guilty? (4:10)

8. What is Cain's punishment from the Lord? (4:11-12)

9. What does Cain think about his punishment? (4:13-14)

10. What do we learn about God in (4:15)?

11. What did Cain do in order to settle in another land? (4:16) What might this say about Cain's relationship with God? Can we learn anything from this story?

WHO IS GOD? WHO AM I?
FROM BAD TO WORSE, WITH A GLIMMER OF HOPE

As time goes by, the world goes from bad to worse. In fact, it gets as evil and bad as it can get. Review Genesis 6:5-8. In the days of Noah, what was the world like? What does God's sorrow and grief say about God? Because of human wickedness, what did God decide to do? Must God destroy evil? Why or why not? What glimmer of hope for mankind appears in this passage?

This Biblical period of ancient history is very sketchy. As evil was increasing upon the earth, there was a glimmer of hope that evil would not totally destroy God's creation. God gives a rundown of Adam's lineage from Adam to Noah (Genesis 5:1-32). That glimmer of hope came through Adam's genealogy which followed the line of Seth. Seth had a son named Enosh and it is said that at that time there began to be those who called upon the name of the Lord (Genesis 4:25-26). Later, in the Adam-Seth lineage, another man named Enoch is said to have walked with God and God took him (Genesis 5:21-24). A couple of generations later, Noah was born, and Noah's father said that Noah would give his family rest from their work, from the difficult toil of their hands due to the ground which the Lord had cursed (Genesis 5:28-32; see Genesis 3:17-19). God will destroy the world that had become an evil beyond saving, but Noah would save the day because he too walked with God and found favor in the eyes of the Lord (Genesis 6:9). The glimmer of hope for a world being ruined by evil was from those who called upon God and walked with God. God's promise in Genesis 3:15 is kept alive until God's salvation is fulfilled in the last book of the Bible.

WALKING WITH GOD

What did "walking with God" mean? People who walk with God are people who call upon the name of the Lord (Genesis 4:26; 12:8; 26:24-25; Psalm 116:12-17; 1 Corinthians 1:2). What is said about these ancient people who walked with God? "Enoch walked with God and he was not, for God took him" (Genesis 5:24). Enoch prophesied, warning the ungodly of God's judgment (Jude 1:14-16). God took him.

BAD NEWS — WHAT WENT WRONG

Notice that he did not live long on the earth as most of the others of that time. God must have taken him to be with him. Can we assume he had eternal life with his God? Noah also walked with God. Of him it was said that he was a righteous man, blameless in his time (Genesis 6:8-9; 7:1). Noah was a man of faith in God who did what God told him to do (Genesis 6:22; Hebrews 11:7). As a result of his faith, he was declared righteous, and he and his family were saved from the judgment of God. Another man who apparently walked with God was a man named Job. We don't know when Job lived. Was it before the flood? Was it in the time of Abraham? Was it before Moses gave us God's law? Based on cultural content in the book, it is possible that he lived in early ancient times.[15] Regardless of when Job lived, what did God say about him? God said he was blameless, upright, fearing God and turning away from evil (Job 1:1, 8; 2:3). Job himself gives a description of what is meant by righteous living (Job, chapter 31).

Were these men self-righteous before God, or was God revealing Himself to them and declaring them as righteous in His sight? God definitely spoke to individuals throughout this period of ancient history. There are clues that God's Spirit was actively involved in the world as a helper of these ancient people. God's Spirit is first mentioned in the Bible as having a part in God's creation (Genesis 1:1-2). During these early days when men and women were multiplying on the face of the earth, God said, "My Spirit shall not strive with man forever" (Genesis 6:3). This must mean that God's Spirit did strive with men, perhaps convicting them of sin through the messages of Enoch and Noah. God did not want anyone to die, which would be in line with God's will and offer of grace for all people. (Ezekiel 18:23, 32). In the case of Job, we have to wonder how Job arrived at such an advanced theology and faith concerning eternal life in the midst of his sufferings (Job 19:25-27).

---

[15] Was Job a real person? Some say poetry implies a mythical person. The use of poetry does not necessarily mean an absence of historical reality. Poetry can be used as much as prose to convey what is true and real. Other Biblical writers refer to Job as a real person (God in Job 40:15; Ezekiel 14:14, 20; James 5:10-11). However, there is no doubt that the spiritual truths being taught in Job are valuable, in spite of what we think about Job's existence.

God must have revealed these things to him. The conclusion is that during times of increasing evil, there were some who walked with God. This provides a glimmer of hope.

THE WORST IS YET TO COME—THE PLACE OF NO RETURN

What is wrong in our lives and in our world is that evil entered. The first man and woman let it enter, and we continue to allow it to enter into our lives and world each day by the bad choices we make. The world we live in offers all kinds of ways for us to make our world a better place, but do you realize that evil will increase all the more as the "end of the world" draws near. The apostle Paul wrote to Timothy: "But realize this, that in the last days difficult times will come. For men will be lovers of self, lovers of money, boastful, arrogant, revilers, disobedient to parents, ungrateful, unholy, unloving, irreconcilable, malicious gossips, without self-control, brutal, haters of good, treacherous, reckless, conceited, lovers of pleasure rather than lovers of God, holding to a form of godliness, although they have denied its power; avoid such men as these" (2 Timothy 3:1-5). In a context of the last days Jesus said lawlessness would increase (Matthew 24:12).

In this chapter "Bad News – What Went Wrong?" we now come to the worst and saddest bad news of all. The saddest thing of all about this world gone wrong is that a person's wrongdoings could lead him or her to a condition called "the second death." God is a patient and loving God who does not want anyone to die (Ezekiel 18:23, 32; 2 Peter 3:9). He does everything He can to help a person come to Him and receive His gift of salvation. However, for any of us who keeps rejecting His offer of mercy, what is said in the Bible can happen, "A man who hardens his heart after much reproof will suddenly be broken beyond remedy" (Proverbs 29:1). God warned Adam that to experience and participate in evil meant he would die. He may not have died physically right away because God wants to give us time for two things. He gives us time to (1) repent, turn to God, and (2) believe God's message of how to be saved. Unfortunately, for many, once a person dies physically, the danger is that of experiencing the second death. The person rejecting God will still be alive, but such a life is not God's eternal life. It is a life of eternal "hell." Jesus warns us of this when he tells people whom they need to fear (Luke 12:4-5). The ultimate death is a condition of being permanently separated from God's future world of righteousness and goodness (Revelation 20:11-15).

The prophet Isaiah warns sinners about the coming of the Day of the Lord: "Behold, the day of the LORD is coming, cruel, with fury and burning anger, to make the land a desolation; and He will exterminate its sinners from it. For the stars of heaven and their constellations will not flash forth their light; the sun will be dark when it rises and the moon will not shed its light. Thus I will punish the world for its evil and the wicked for their iniquity; I will also put an end to the arrogance of the proud and abase the haughtiness of the ruthless" (Isaiah 13:9-11). When that day comes, we will be near the time of no return. Thankfully, God has warned us so that we could still have time to avoid God's coming day of judgment.

This brings us to the closing of this chapter on why we no longer portray the image of God-likeness in our lives. God created everything good but evil entered the world. We do not need to go far for us to see that our world has many degrees of evil. Evil is in what individuals consider to be minor wrongdoings, and it extends to wrongs depicting humanity's most horrific treatment of other humans. We can see it every day in televised news reports, as well as from other types of media. We also experience various degrees of evil in our own lives. Because of a world gone bad, God and each of us must now deal with the world's imperfections, including the unbelievable horrors committed by mankind against one another. Plus, we also have the evils of nature to contend with.

GOD'S LOVE GUARANTEES THAT ALL IS NOT LOST

Is there any hope for the restoration of a good world, and for our reconciliation to God, and God-likeness? God offers grace and a future fantastic life to all who will respond. "God did not send His Son into the world to judge the world, but that the world might be saved through Him" (John 3:16-18). The way to escape ultimate death is found

WHO IS GOD? WHO AM I?

throughout the Bible. That's what God's written book is all about. It is God's story of how God created a good world, how it went bad, and how God's sovereign plan is unfolding to restore it to being good again. God warns all of us to not harden our hearts, but to exercise faith in His message of good news (Read Hebrews 4:1-7). The thought of being eternally separated from God, in a tormenting place of no return, is a scary thought. This thought, for many people, contradicts their view of God as a loving God. Many do not want to think or hear about such a thing. I don't blame them. I come out of a life of fearfulness, and although fear can be helpful, it's not a pleasant feeling. To some degree, fear is crippling in everyone's life. It can control us and prevent us from discovering and enjoying what a good life has to offer. In the next chapter, we shall focus on the good news about God, us, and our future.

Chapter 7

GOOD NEWS ABOUT GOD, US, AND OUR FUTURE

The previous chapter can be very disturbing and hard for people to read. The hard truth is that every person who has ever been born into this world has been born into a realm of death. There are many reminders of this truth all around us. Our news media shows people dying from wars and bombings, from murders and shootings, from terrible accidents, and from nature's floods, fires, earthquakes, tornados, and hurricanes. Many people we know are dying from a disease of some kind. And, we pass by cemeteries reminding us that death comes to all persons. Scientists would love to find a cure for all sicknesses and death. Good news! There is a God who can accomplish this. How does God do it?

God's good news was announced long ago to a group of common shepherds tending their flocks of sheep. An angel from God appeared to them to give them the news. God saves us by sending a person. In the Bible, a physician named Luke tells us about this event. Luke writes, "But the angel said to them, "Do not be afraid; for behold, I bring you good news of great joy which will be for all the people; for today in the city of David there has been born for you a Savior, who is Christ the Lord" (Luke 2:10-11). He saves us.

GOD'S GRACE

God is a just God who judges and punishes wrongdoing. But God is also, and above all, a God of love. Along with punishing the guilty, God proclaimed this about who He is, "The LORD, the LORD God, compassionate and gracious, slow to anger, and abounding in lovingkindness and truth, who keeps lovingkindness for thousands, who forgives iniquity, transgression and sin" (Exodus 34:6-7). All through the Bible, parts of this description of God's grace are noted—for example, Psalm 40:11; Nehemiah 9:17; Joel 2:13.

WHO IS GOD? WHO AM I?

Let's revisit the entire chapter of Genesis 3:1-24, considering ways God demonstrates His compassion, grace and mercy.

1. What does God give man and woman freedom to do (3:1-7)? Why do you think God gives them freedom to choose? What do you think a relationship with God and one another would be like without free will?[16]

2. How do you think God was showing mercy to the man and woman by visiting and calling them out? (3:8-13)

3. What hope does God give the human race by His words to Satan (3:15)?

4. What compassion does God show the man and woman by letting them live, have a family, and do work (3:16-19)? To answer this, consider again God's definition of His character in Exodus 34:6-7. Why would God not bring death upon them immediately? (see Ezekiel 18:23, 32; 33:10-15; 2 Pet. 3:9)

5. How would it show Adam and Eve that God is loving them by clothing them (3:21)?

GOD'S DILEMMA AND OURS

How can God love and forgive people, when He must punish the guilty? When we humans commit a crime and are found guilty in a court of law, the judge cannot say, "I love you, you are free to go." People would be upset. If justice is not done, the people who have been wronged, who feel violated and unsafe, and who have suffered a loss

---

[16] Michael Egnor and Denyse O'Leary, "The Immortal Mind" (Worthy Hatchette Bood Group, New York, 2025). This book says that free will is something many scientists and neuroscientists deny, claiming that humans do not have free will, that everything is determined by the brain and/or life's preceding events. In Chapter 8 titled, "Free Will Is a Real and Intrinsic Part of the Soul", the author gives reasons to affirm free will, pgs. 135-150.

due to the crime, would be outraged. They would cry out, "This is not right, they need to pay for what they have done. Thus, how can God, and we too, love people when they deserve justice? Forgiveness and justice seem to cancel each other out. But do they?

The apostle Paul wrestled with the problems caused by evil's invasion into God's good world, especially evil's invasion into his own life. Paul said, "I find then the principle that evil is present in me, the one who wants to do good" (Romans 7:21). This caused him to ask the question all of us must answer, "Wretched man that I am! Who will set me free from the body of this death" (Romans 7:24)? How could Paul be loved and forgiven when the sins he was guilty of committing needed to be punished? Paul was under God's wrath and was subject to God's punishment. The answer to Paul's dilemma was Jesus' death on the cross. There Jesus dealt with both love and justice. Jesus' death satisfied God's wrath against Paul's sin, thus freeing God to be able to offer him forgiveness and eternal life. The cross of Jesus is God's great good news for all people. God loves people who deserve justice by sending Jesus to pay the penalty for their wrongs.

Here are words Paul wrote from God to explain this truth. "But God demonstrates His own love toward us, in that while we were yet sinners, Christ died for us. Much more then, having now been justified (*declared not guilty*) by His blood, we shall be saved from the wrath of God through Him" (Romans 5:8-9). "Now I make known to you, brethren, the gospel which I preached to you, which also you received, in which also you stand, by which also you are saved, if you hold fast the word which I preached to you, unless you believed in vain. For I delivered to you as of first importance what I also received, that Christ died for our sins according to the Scriptures, and that He was buried, and that He was raised on the third day according to the Scriptures" (1 Corinthians 15:1-4). "For I am not ashamed of the gospel, for it is the power of God for salvation to everyone who believes, to the Jew first and also to the Greek" (Romans 1:16). "For the wages of sin is death, but the free gift of God is eternal life in Christ Jesus our Lord" (Romans 6:23). Justice is not needed in a perfect world where there is no wrongdoing. But through the freedom of our will, evil has been allowed to enter our world. Now justice is necessary. But can God's love allow evil to destroy what is good? Can love allow evil to destroy our lives? My life? God has a way to not let evil destroy us. From the beginning to the end of God's salvation, it is all by God's grace. We cannot save ourselves, but He can.

PEOPLE TRAPPED IN THIS CORRUPTED WORLD NEED GOD'S GOOD NEWS

Let me share an example of how evil's entrance into our world destroys human life, causing our path to death. I know a number of persons who are trying to overcome their past lives of physical or sexual abuse, rejection, shame, and guilt. What can heal them of a lifetime of pain, failure, beatings, rejection, and regrets? Such experiences haunt their memories, and those feelings never go away. Trying to stay busy so one does not think about it, or justifying what happened, does not keep the memories from resurfacing. For many, the life they experience in this world is depressing and overwhelming. They may have tried lots of things to fix themselves, but nothing was successful. There is something deeper going on that prevents them from experiencing victory over the evils that are destroying them. They have not been loved by people they should have been able to trust. All they've known is rejection and messages telling them, "You are no good." Their attempts to have friends, or to enter into loving and lasting relationships have failed. They have been hurt, they are hurting, and because of it, they keep hurting others. Their failures only reconfirm that they are no good. How can a person be helped to accept themselves when there is this deep belief that he or she is not loveable? If someone does try to love them, they have a hard time trusting that love. Deep within are these thoughts, "I cannot believe that another person could love me. Even if I try to have a relationship, I will fail them at some point and I will be rejected again. Who I am as a bad person will eventually disappoint them, and they will have reason not to love me." The final conclusion in this person's mind is, "I cannot change, and I am not worth loving." One of the meanings of being a divided person is that the evil within us is fighting the good we desire. The war within us makes us broken and without peace. If we are honest, at some point, evil is destroying all of us. In some way we are all dying.

WHAT IT MEANS FOR GOD TO CLOTHE US

To help people with their insurmountable problems and self-destructive thinking, Genesis 3:21, comes to mind. I have said to individuals, and to myself, "Obviously, letting go of your past and living a life of love, happiness, and peace is not something you can do. I don't think God wants you to keep trying to help yourself." I think it shocks a person to hear this. Such a thought goes against people's advice that they need to get counselling so they can move on. Human counselling can be very helpful, but if it lacks truths that only God can add, it can prove to not be enough. We are enslaved to the fears and wrongdoing and death that surround us; enslaved to wrongdoing that cannot be overcome. How can someone, like is described above, who has not been loved, come to believe in love, especially God's love? Back to Genesis 3:21, "The Lord God made garments of skin for Adam and his wife, and clothed them." I'm sure God clothed Adam and Eve with physical clothing, but could it have also provided a spiritual clue that God's plan to redeem us includes the sacrifice of another's life? There is seemingly something deeper in the mind of God as He graciously clothes Adam and Eve. Just as an animal had to die to provide clothing for Adam and Eve, God already knew in His mind that His Son would die for their sin so they could be clothed with acceptance and forgiveness (Ephesians 1:3-7). God's clothing of Adam and Eve was a practical way to show them that, in spite of their sin, He still loved them and could save them. Yes, we need to do what Genesis 3:21 says. We need to let God clothe us. Then, we can come to know and believe God's love for us (1 John 4:16).

WHAT JESUS DOES TO MAKE IT POSSIBLE FOR US TO BE NEWLY CLOTHED

As was pointed out above, God's love is demonstrated by His Son dying for the sinner. In doing so, he takes the sinners punishment of death, which enables God's forgiveness. But there is something else

WHO IS GOD? WHO AM I?

that needs to be considered. God cannot allow sinful behaviors in the world to continue to destroy what is good. People need to be loved and accepted, but they cannot continue in sin just because they are forgiven. To become unified, our divided self must become healed and whole. God's goal is to restore us to His image, to become like God in our character and in how we live our lives each day. For this to happen, we must learn to put off our old clothing and put on God's new clothing (Ephesians 4:22-24). An analogy to this might be to note that when God clothed Adam and Eve, in order to put on the new clothing God gave them, they needed to put off the leaves that they had used to make their own clothing (Genesis 3:7). Yes, salvation is something Jesus did for us on the cross so that we could be forgiven, but salvation is an ongoing process of becoming the person God created us to be, a person who is like God in character and oneness.

Returning to the example I used above concerning persons trapped in this corrupted world, whose lives have been destroyed by sinful ways, let us consider how Jesus enables them to be healed and be whole again by being restored to the image of God. It begins with God revealing Himself and His truth to them. This causes or draws them to consider their broken life and their need for a savior. In response to His grace in sending a message, if they yield to God's message, God can enter into their lives by His Holy Spirit and continue His work to save and restore them. Still, it may not be easy for them to overcome their feelings of worthlessness, being unloved, and being without the hope of change. Change may happen more quickly in some than others, but many, because of their past, do not find it easy to learn to trust and love others. But as they learn God's truths and are enabled to believe them, they are gradually changed. With God's help, by growing to believe His promises, and by practicing His teachings, they are being healed. There is something more. An important part of their being able to believe God loves them, and to overcome their lack of trust in people, is to experience the genuine caring love of persons around them. That is where the church, God's people, is very important to their healing. We are to love and accept one another as Christ has loved and accepted us. In doing so, those who have not been loved and accepted can be changed so they can begin to trust and love others, which is something they want and need to be able to do. We all need to love and be loved, and it happens because God first loved us so that we could be freed from our past to love others (1 John 4:19-21). Even as a Christian, we will go through struggles and pain, but God is present to help us to keep learning and growing to become like Jesus our Lord (Romans 8:28-29).

A PRACTICAL PROBLEM WE ALL FACE

People often find it difficult to love and accept others, if at the same time, they feel like they are condoning their sinful behaviors. How do you convince people that you love and accept them, and yet not condone their wrongdoing? This is a tough thing to learn. This is one reason why Jesus tells us to love our enemies. It is how they can come to know God loves them. But if I do love them, they could still hate me, reject me, and kill me. It is risky to love. We fear rejection and the pain it can bring us. That is what Jesus endured by loving others. He must be willing to die for them to show them his love. That is what we too must learn to be willing to do. Putting off our old selves and putting on a new self requires a kind of death to self (John 12:24-25; Luke 9:22-24). Life comes out of death.

I read about a school-teacher who wanted to find a way to help his students willingly change their bad behaviors in class. The standard practice in those days was to punish the students for their bad behavior. The punishment was physical, perhaps a spanking or slaps on the hand. One day, he got an idea which all the other teachers thought was ridiculous. Whenever a student badly misbehaved in class, he would have the student come forward. The students were surprised when the teacher reversed the punishment. He gave him or her the wooden ruler and told them to hit him hard across his knuckles. They didn't want to do it, but he insisted. It didn't take long for the attitudes and behaviors of the students to change. Kids stopped bullying other kids and making fun of them and stopped resisting the teacher's rules. Everyone appreciated a controlled and pleasant classroom. What caused them to change? No one wanted to hurt their teacher, especially knowing they themselves deserved the punishment, not him.

WHO IS GOD? WHO AM I?

Dying for others to convince them of your love. Wow! That's hard. But I have discovered how it works. When I realize that another suffers my punishment and forgives me, specifically Jesus, it makes me want to change my behavior from bad to good. We may have a problem of repeating the same sins over and over, perhaps we have an addiction of some kind. Here's how it works. Each time we sin; we ask God's forgiveness so we can feel better by His acceptance. One day, the thought may occur to us, "How can God keep forgiving me when I keep hurting Him by my wrongdoing?" When we realize that we are hurting God by doing wrong, but that He willingly took my punishment for me, I suddenly realized that I don't want to keep hurting the one who loves me that much. It doesn't seem right to hurt the one who suffered for me. We are the cause of His suffering. Even though he was willing to suffer for me and keep forgiving me, it broke my heart. I couldn't keep hurting him. I couldn't keep doing wrong, thinking I will be forgiven. I had to take seriously my need to change my attitude and my addictive behavior. What glorifies God the most is for us to become like He is, and to do His will. His will is to accomplish the work He has given each of us to do. That is how Jesus glorified God His Father (John 14:9-12; 17:4-5).

GOD KNOWS WHEN TO DO WHAT TO HELP SOMEONE CHANGE

God's love is amazing. We need it. Love heals us. But we can't ignore that God hates wickedness and evil and that God must punish the guilty. As Christians, how do we handle God's discipline and correction? What do we think about God's justice and punishment? Those things we don't like. And so, we need to learn how to view those things correctly in our understanding of how God operates and how we are to treat ourselves and others who are guilty. We live in a world where justice must be administered as needed. Justice is necessary for a healthy society to exist. Justice is not only about punishment of wrongs but often involves mercy in meeting needs. Justice is a part of who God is. God calls us to perform His justice in our daily lives (Micah 6:8; Isaiah 1:16-17; Acts 4:32-35). Do we allow evil to continue? When do we discipline and correct, when do we punish, or when do we allow evil to run its course? When and how do we step into a situation to help someone being wronged? Not easy situations to work out. We need God's wisdom. When confronted with the meaning of the cross of Jesus, we have a choice. We can run from doing what he wants us to do, blame him for the bad things that happen, or, we can take responsibility for our attitudes and actions, repent, respect him, and obey him. Love, acceptance, and doing good for others, as God does, can win many people over (Romans 2:4; 2 Timothy 2:21-26). But it may also be true that confrontation or punishment wins them over (1 Timothy 5:20; 1 Corinthians 5:9-13). If people admit they deserve it, it may lead to repentance (Luke 13:1-5). How do we know when to do what, when to be soft or to be hard? God knows. Maybe that is why He does not always punish evil right away, knowing that some people need one thing and others need something else. Plus, God is patient, not wishing anyone perish and giving time to repent. Wisdom knows what to do when. Many will not want to hear about Christ. Many persist in their wickedness (John 3:36). In that case, to provide for a safe world, justice and punishment are necessary.

CHANGING WORLDS

We need to escape this world of destructive evils that are both outside of us and within us. We need to escape God's judgment and punishment that we know we deserve. We need to change worlds. We need to come out of this world and be transferred into another world, a world of peace and goodness, a world of God's making. We need to leave the world that we live in and be made citizens of another world. This is the great miracle of God, to transfer us from this world into the world of God's Son, Jesus. It is through His Son that God rescues us from a dark and dying world. Jesus came and lived among us. He was a part of this divided and dying world. He knows that everything needs to be made new. It is because of Jesus, the Christ, that we are enabled to be unified with self, others, and nature. Jesus is our greatest good news and the primary unifying factor we all need. He claimed to be "the way, the truth, and the life" (John 14:6). He is a truly amazing person. There has never been, nor ever will there be, anyone like him. By changing worlds, I am not saying we are to physically leave the world we live in. We are in the world, but we are not to be of the world. (read John 17: 14-16; Romans 12:2; 1 Corinthians 5:9-10; 1 John 2:15-17). We must leave the evil ways of the world we live in, be more like Jesus, and minister God's love and mercy to those in this world in a way that helps them see and want Jesus.

WHAT IT MEANS TO CHANGE WORLDS.

(1) Jesus used the word "converted" in Matthew 18:3. It means to change one thing into another. For example, you can convert a pretty stone into a ring. We must be converted from a dying life to an eternal life. We must be converted from this world into another world. That world is the kingdom of heaven, the kingdom of God. (2) In Colossians 1:13 the word "transferred" is used to say that God rescues us from the domain of darkness, transferring us into the kingdom of His beloved Son. (3) Jesus uses the words "born again" (John 3:3-6) to say that a new birth enables us to enter into the kingdom of God. (4) "Citizenship" is another word. It tells us we are no longer to be citizens of this world, but to become citizens of another world. "So then you are no longer strangers and aliens, but you are fellow citizens with the saints and members of the household of God" (Ephesians 2:19). To be citizens in another world means we live under the authorities and laws of that world. "This world is passing away, and its lusts; but the one who does the will of God lives forever" (1 John 2:17). (5) To change worlds means we are given a "new heart" that causes its citizens to want to obey the authorities and laws of God's world (Ezekiel 36:24-27) God knows that people need a "new heart" to happily live in His world (Deuteronomy 5:29). (6) The Bible describes changing worlds this way: we have become a "new creation", the old has passed and the new has come (2 Corinthians 5:17). Jesus himself said, "My kingdom is not of this world…My kingdom is not of this realm" (John 18:36). The Bible says, "Do not love the world nor the things in the world. If anyone loves the world, the love of the Father is not in him" (1 John 2:15). God meant for us to love and enjoy the earth He originally made for us, but

we are not to love the world as it now is, a world corrupted by human's sinful lusts (1 John 2:16). The word "world" means the world that is infected with evil. Because people are also infected with the evil effects of sin, we must change worlds. What Jesus did makes it possible for us to be saved by changing worlds. We change worlds by letting God clothe us with His garments (Genesis 3:21).

WHAT IT MEANS FOR GOD TO CLOTHE US

Besides physical clothing, Which God used with Adam and Eve, being clothed is a metaphor that God uses in scripture for spiritual clothing. Isaiah 61:10 says, "I will rejoice greatly in the Lord, my soul will exalt in my God; for He has clothed me with garments of salvation, He has wrapped me with a robe of righteousness...." How is this clothing from God attained, who can attain it, and what blessing does it bring to us? The apostle Paul recognized this need for God's clothing in his own life. Paul was a very religious person. By obeying God's rules and laws, he was relying on his own good works to save him. But after Jesus appeared to him and told him he was looking in the wrong places to be saved, he realized that instead of relying on his own righteousness to save him, he needed Jesus to clothe him with "the righteousness that comes from God on the basis of faith" (Philippians 3:7-11). The Old Testament father of our faith, Abraham, also learned this truth (read Romans 4:1-8). Once we receive God's gift of righteousness, we are to put off our old way of living and put on God's new way of living. The Bible puts it this way, "in reference to your former manner of life, you lay aside the old self, which is being corrupted in accordance with the lusts of deceit, and that you be renewed in the spirit of your mind, and put on the new self which in God has been created in holiness and righteousness of the truth" (Ephesians 4:22-24). Not only is God enabling us to change our clothes, He will change the earth's clothes as well (Psalm 102:25-26), giving us a new home.

WHO IS GOD? WHO AM I?
GOOD NEWS ABOUT WHO I AM

We have already established that we are created to be in God's image and to reflect who God is. When we become a follower of Jesus, God's goal for us, which is to be our goal as well, is to grow in looking and being like Jesus (Romans 8:29). A book written by a relatively unknown woman focuses on who we are as a believer in Christ. Noreen Sergent reminds us of the importance of knowing and believing who we are according to God's word. She says in her book, "Don't drag yourself down with the words you say about yourself; build yourself up with what God says about you." She continues, "So whom are you listening to? Are you listening to what God says about you? Or are you listening to what you say about yourself or what somebody else says about you?"[17]

I don't know about you, but I sometimes believe things about myself that make me feel depressed. Things like "you are lazy, you never follow through with what you know you should do." Or "you don't really care about others, you think only of yourself," or "you are afraid of everything, and you try and control your life to protect yourself instead of trusting God." Don't get me wrong, it is good to listen to criticisms of yourself, especially from God and others, because we can't change things if we don't know about them. But if we dwell on those things, they can drive us to destructive thoughts and despair that is not good for us. Critical thoughts we have about ourselves may be true, but actually, they may not be as true as we think. Maybe, more than we realize, we have made progress in overcoming our weaknesses. However, all of us can experience healing when we come to see ourselves, not as we see us, but as God sees us. Believing what God says about who we are in Christ is great good news; news that makes a difference in our self-worth and in giving us strength to live a new and godly life. We must counter thoughts that condemn us with the things God says about us. Yes, we must also recognize our weaknesses and shortcomings and be seeking God to help us change, but we can't give

---

[17] Noreen Sergent, Just Who Do You Say Yor Are; A Word Study of Who God Says You Are (Creation House Press, Lake Mary, Florida, 2013), pgs. 84-86.

GOOD NEWS ABOUT GOD

in to becoming depressed over them. God wants to help us with our weaknesses, and He knows more than we do about what we need in order to change. The Holy Spirit is an inner guide and help with this. I know that I can't change into godlikeness on my own. I need all the means He can give me to help me become a mature believer and faithful follower of Jesus.

We must keep on growing to be like Jesus and make that our motivation for change. When we change worlds, we are living by the principles of the new world we have moved into. We are persons who are precious in the sight of God. He will continue to forgive and accept us and work in us to grow us into His likeness (Philippians 1:6). Praise His name! When you read the Bible, be sure to notice what God says about you as a member of His family. Reading the book of Ephesians and underlining or writing down everything you come across that says who you are as a believer in Christ is a good place to start.

To glorify God is one of our main purposes in life. When it comes to how we glorify God, I have told people to look at nature for what it can teach us. Look at a tree. That tree is glorifying God. "How" you may ask? It is glorifying God by simply being what God created it to be. It is giving off oxygen to help our breathing. It is filtering carbon dioxide out of the air, eliminating a gas harmful to our health. It provides shade to help keep us cool. It provides wood from which we can build our house. That is how we glorify God, by being like that tree, by simply becoming and being who God created us to be. Peter once said to Jesus, "We have left everything to follow you; what then will there be for us? Is it worth following Jesus? Read on to see.

WHAT IS THE GOOD NEWS ABOUT OUR FUTURE

1. WE HAVE A GUARANTEED HOPE. Hope is the certainty that what God has promised will happen. It is not wishing it will happen, but knowing it will happen because God said so, and He is faithful to keep His word. On this road of adventure we are travelling we can look forward to the coming kingdom of God. During his lifetime on earth, Jesus preached about the kingdom of God everywhere he went (Matthew 4:17; Mark 1:14-15). By things he said and did, Jesus was

giving a glimpse of what his coming kingdom will be like. Jesus went about loving people and doing good, including many miracles (Acts 10:38). When he did miracles, or had his disciples do miracles, the point was to be made that the kingdom was at hand or had come near (Matthew 10:7; Luke 10:9). Healing the sick, the blind, the crippled, raising the dead, calming nature's storms, and casting out demons demonstrated that none of those harmful conditions that are a part of this sinful world are present in the future kingdom of God. In God's kingdom there is no more pain or suffering or death (Revelation 21:3-4). When Jesus' followers came back to report to Jesus about all the miracles they did in his name, he told them not to rejoice in the miracles so much, but to rejoice that their names are written in heaven (Luke 10:17-20). Eternal life is not something future only but begins now when we receive Christ into our lives (John 17:3). This is why Jesus emphasizes for us to "seek first the kingdom and his righteousness (Matthew 6:33). That is why Jesus was so eager to have people repent and receive him, so they could enter his kingdom. To those who believe, Jesus sends His Holy Spirit to be in them as a helper and to give them a taste of the joyful spirit of life in his kingdom (Romans 14:17). One way the Holy Spirit helps us is to give us a changed heart so we would have a heart like the "heart" of his kingdom, full of compassion, mercy, forgiveness, and doing good for all those around us (Galatians 6:9; Titus 2:11-14, 3:14). The reason Jesus taught us to love (John 13:34-35) is because in his kingdom, love is the "standard procedure" for all our relationships. The future God has planned for those who believe in Him is called our living hope (1 Peter 1:3). Having a glimpse and an experience of what his kingdom is like helps prepare us for what we will inherit in the future.

2. WE WILL RECEIVE AN INHERITANCE. 1 Peter 1:3-4 says we have an inheritance that will not fade away and that is reserved in heaven for us. Not much is said about what that inheritance involves, but Jesus said we are to store up treasures in heaven rather than on earth. We store up treasures in heaven by serving Christ and doing the good works the Lord wants us to do (Acts 20:35; Colossians 3:23-24; 1 Timothy 6:17-19). What do we inherit? We inherit eternal life (Matthew 19:29). We inherit the kingdom of God (Matthew 25:34; James 2:5).

GOOD NEWS ABOUT GOD

We inherit the earth (Matthew 5:5), and the world (Romans 4:13). We don't choose our inheritance. God chooses it for us (Psalm 47:4). We are fellow heirs with Christ (Romans 8:16-17) and we can't imagine the things God has prepared for those who love Him (1 Corinthians 2:9). For one thing, God is creative. That means to be created in his image means we too are creative. There will be lots of satisfying creativity and work to do in the next life.

3. WE ARE BLESSED WITH A NEW BODY AND A NEW EARTH. In the beginning God created a physical world that was real and good. God meant for the spiritual and the physical to be forever in harmony with each other. That has not changed. Even though this corrupted world will pass away, God will restore all things and remake a good world (Psalm 102:25-26; Acts 3:19-21). In the future, God does not separate the spiritual from the physical. We will have new physical bodies (Romans 8:11; Colossians 3:21; Luke 24:37-39; 1 Corinthians 15:50-54), and we will live on a new earth (Isaiah 65:17; 66:22).

4. WE ESCAPE GOD'S JUDGMENT OF CONDEMNATION. When Jesus died on the cross to pay for our sin, through faith in Him, we are declared righteous (1 Peter 2:24; Romans 4:5-8). It's like going to court and standing before the judge to be tried for our wrongs. Being found guilty, we are sentenced to be punished for the wrongs we have done. But because Jesus paid for our sins by suffering our punishment of death for us, we are declared not guilty. There is now no condemnation for those in Christ Jesus (Romans 8:1). When we believe in Jesus and decide to follow him and his ways, this means that in the last judgment, when people face God, and those who have not believed in Christ are sentenced to life in hell; no worries, we have escaped that judgment (Revelation 20:11-15). There is another judgment, however, that Christians will attend. It is called the judgment seat of Christ. Instead of standing before a court to be judged for our sins, good news, it is a time of being rewarded for what we have done for Christ (2 Corinthians 5:10; Colossians 3:23-24). However, we do not escape being held accountable for how we have lived our lives in service to our Lord and Savior. Is this something to fear? Not if we have loved him and served him faithfully and willingly out of love. Our motive for obeying and serving Christ is not to gain rewards from him, but rather

WHO IS GOD? WHO AM I?

our motive comes from a purified heart of love that willingly wants to do his will (1 Timothy 1:5). We don't obey Christ's teachings out of duty to earn his approval. Instead, we want to live as Christ teaches. If this is our approach to living the Christian life, we will have no fear, only gladness and the expectation of "well done good and faithful servant" (1 John 4:15-19; 1 Corinthians 3:12-15; Matthew 10:42).

5. WE WILL REIGN WITH CHRIST ON THIS EARTH. Jesus taught his disciples how to pray. One of the things he told them to pray for was this, "Your kingdom come, your will be done, on earth as it is in heaven" (Matthew 6:10). This has been interpreted by the church in a number of ways. (1) "Your kingdom come on earth as it is in heaven" means that the church, under the leadership of Christ, will enable his kingdom to come on earth by converting people to Christ so that all governments and people on earth will submit to the church's authority and rule. At different times, the church has tried to force people's conversions and has threatened rulers to submit to the church's leaders or be kicked out of the church and thus be condemned to hell. Even today, the church has not made visible headway in bringing the world under the authority of Jesus Christ. Evil seemingly rules. (2) Others have interpreted the prayer to mean that the kingdom of God is a spiritual kingdom with Christ ruling the world from heaven through changing people's hearts so that we are presently reigning with him by doing His work in this world. (3) Many point out that the Bible seems to clearly say that Jesus will physically come to earth, that the world will yield to him as king, that his kingdom will do away with all war and create a world of peace, and Christ's people will reign with him (Acts 1:6-11; Zechariah 14:1-9; Micah 4:1-3; Daniel 7:13-14, 27; Isaiah 65:17-25; Revelation 5:9-10; 20:4-6). This interpretation says Israel will still have a key part to play at the end of this age and all the promises God made to Israel will be fulfilled. Of course, others disagree, saying the promises have already been fulfilled or negated, saying Israel has gone against God and has given up its place to the church, who now are God's people. There will be no kingdom on earth, rather God's kingdom is a spiritual kingdom from heaven where Christ rules over the hearts of his people. Heaven, not earth is where the kingdom resides. In light of all these interpretations concerning the

prayer for "God's kingdom to come on earth as it is in heaven," you and I are left to decide based on our conviction concerning what the Bible teaches to be the truth. At any rate, the fact that the Bible says his people will reign with him implies that believers in Jesus will be given tasks to perform in his kingdom (see for example, Matthew 19:27-28; 1 Corinthians 6:2-3). Some believe that God will give tasks to volunteers in his coming earthly kingdom (Psalm 110:1-3). Perhaps those tasks will be given to believers who have faithfully practiced what God has given and gifted them to do in their lifetime on our current earth (Matthew 24:42-47; 25:14-21). It doesn't matter which of the three interpretations you believe, it all ends up in the same place. No saying "I'm right, you are wrong" needed.

6. WE WILL ENJOY RELATIONSHIPS WITH LOVED ONES. When believers in Jesus are raised from the dead, they receive new bodies and are "caught up together" in the clouds to meet the Lord in the air, and so they shall always be with the Lord (1 Thessalonians 4:13-18). When King David's baby died, he commented that his son would not return but that he would go to meet his son in the future (2 Samuel 12:23). Jesus once told people that a day would come when people would come from various places and will be able to meet with Abraham, Isaac, and Jacob in the kingdom of heaven (Matthew 8:11). Obviously, verses like these tell us that we will be with, see, and know people in God's coming kingdom. We are fellow citizens (Philippians 3:20).

7. WE WILL NO LONGER HAVE TO BATTLE AGAINST SIN AND EVIL. It will be a good and righteous world. We will live in a world where God creates all things new. (Revelation 21:4-5). In this world, there is war between our fleshly nature and our spiritual nature. That will be gone. In the next world, we will have what the Bible calls a spiritual body (1 Corinthians 15:42-44). It is a body that no longer sins, but one that will perfectly love and be in harmony with God, all people, and all things. Our salvation is thus completed when we are delivered from all sin, pain, and death. All will finally be in complete unity and peace.

WHO IS GOD? WHO AM I?

NEXT CHAPTER: Eternal Life - what it means, how to get it, and how we know we have it. The Bible says, "But whoever drinks of the water that I will give him will never be thirsty again. The water that I will give him will become in him a spring of water welling up to eternal life" (John 4:14).

Chapter 8

WHAT THE BIBLE SAYS ABOUT ETERNAL LIFE

SEGMENT ONE
WHERE ETERNAL LIFE COMES FROM

Read Genesis 1:1. Who is this God who created the heavens and the earth? Psalm 90:2 – "Before the mountains were born or You gave birth to the earth and the world, even from everlasting to everlasting, You are God."

What does the Psalm writer say about God?

_____

_____

Read Psalm 102:25-27 — "Of old You founded the earth, and the heavens are the work of Your hands. Even they will perish, but You endure; and all of them will wear out like a garment; like clothing You will change them, and they will be changed. But You are the same, and Your years will not come to an end."

What does the Psalm writer say about God?

_____

_____

Read Isaiah 43:10b-11 – "Before Me there was no God formed, and there will be none after Me. "I, even I, am the LORD, and there is no savior besides Me."

WHO IS GOD? WHO AM I?

What does God say about Himself in Isaiah 43:10b-11?

_____
_____
_____

COMMENT: The Bible claims that God is self-existing, without beginning or end. The Bible says that God is before all things that exist in this world, and He will continue even if all things cease to exist. Why must God be the source of eternal life?

_____
_____

FOLLOWING IS THE STORY OF A MAN WHO CAME TO JESUS TO ASK ABOUT ETERNAL LIFE.

Read Mark 10:17-22 — "As He was setting out on a journey, a man ran up to Him and knelt before Him, and asked Him, 'Good Teacher, what shall I do to inherit eternal life?' And Jesus said to him, 'Why do you call Me good? No one is good except God alone. You know the commandments, 'DO NOT MURDER, DO NOT COMMIT ADULTERY, DO NOT STEAL, DO NOT BEAR FALSE WITNESS, Do not defraud, HONOR YOUR FATHER AND MOTHER.' And he said to Him, 'Teacher, I have kept all these things from my youth up.' Looking at him, Jesus felt a love for him and said to him, 'One thing you lack: go and sell all you possess and give to the poor, and you will have treasure in heaven; and come, follow Me.' But at these words he was saddened, and he went away grieving, for he was one who owned much property."

Why do you think this man came to Jesus and then walked away from a chance to get eternal life?

_____
_____

Do you fear death? Why or why not? What do you believe about eternal life? Have you ever thought about dying and what happens after

WHAT THE BIBLE SAYS ABOUT ETERNAL LIFE

you die? How important is it to you that you have eternal life, and to know for sure that you have it?

JESUS DEFINES ETERNAL LIFE

John 17:3 — "This is eternal life, that they may know You, the only true God, and Jesus Christ whom You have sent." How does Jesus define eternal life?

THOSE WHO PERSONALLY KNEW JESUS AGREED WITH HIS DEFINITION OF ETERNAL LIFE

1 John 1:1-3 – "What was from the beginning, what we have heard, what we have seen with our eyes, what we have looked at and touched with our hands, concerning the Word of Life—and the life was manifested, and we have seen and testify and proclaim to you the eternal life, which was with the Father and was manifested to us—what we have seen and heard we proclaim to you also, so that you too may have fellowship with us; and indeed our fellowship is with the Father, and with His Son Jesus Christ." (Underline the word "proclaim" that appears two times above. See questions 1 & 2 below)

(1) In 1 John 1:1-2, What are the disciples proclaiming about Jesus Christ, which was manifested to us?

(2) In verse 3, What is the reason they give for proclaiming the eternal life?

WHO IS GOD? WHO AM I?

COMMENT: Notice how Jesus defines eternal life. It is not only about a forever duration of time, but about a quality relationship. Eternal life is knowing and having meaningful and continual fellowship with the God who is eternal life. This relationship begins in this life by spending time with him (Revelation 3:20).

Genesis 1:27 – "God created man in His own image, in the image of God He created him; male and female He created them." Genesis 2:7 - "Then the LORD God formed man of dust from the ground, and breathed into his nostrils the breath of life; and man became a living being." Consider Genesis 2:16-17.

Do you think God originally created mankind to live forever? Why do you think so?

_____
_____

What have you learned in segment one about eternal life and where eternal life comes from?

_____
_____

The next segment shows us why humans need eternal life.

SEGMENT TWO
HOW DEATH ENTERED OUR LIVES AND WORLD

Genesis 2:15-17 — "Then the LORD God took the man and put him into the garden of Eden to cultivate it and keep it. The LORD God commanded the man, saying, 'From any tree of the garden you may eat freely; but from the tree of the knowledge of good and evil you shall not eat, for in the day that you eat from it you will surely die.'"

COMMENT: Originally, humans had God's everlasting life. But something happened that explains why we now need eternal life.

Genesis 3:6, 9-10 — "When the woman saw that the tree was good for food, and that it was a delight to the eyes, and that the tree was desirable to make one wise, she took from its fruit and ate; and she gave

WHAT THE BIBLE SAYS ABOUT ETERNAL LIFE

also to her husband with her, and he ate...." "Then the LORD God called to the man, and said to him, 'Where are you?' He said, 'I heard the sound of You in the garden, and I was afraid because I was naked; so I hid myself.'"

What happened to separate the man and woman from God so that they now needed to regain His eternal life?

_____
_____
_____

What do you think the man and woman could have done to get back on God's side again?

_____
_____
_____

COMMENT: God told man he would surely die if he did something that God told him not to do. But the man and woman chose their own way to live, not God's way, thus separating themselves from God. This fact is seen when God came to visit them in the garden. They hid from God and did not want to meet Him. By choosing their own way to live, and not God's way, they still had life, but not God's kind of life. Their goodness became corrupted with evil. Apart from God, in whom there is no evil, they would die. To regain God's kind of life means to get reconnected and enter back into a right relationship with God.

THE FOLLOWING BIBLE VERSES POINT OUT WHY WE NEED ETERNAL LIFE

Ephesians 2:1-5, 12 – "And you were dead in your trespasses and sins, in which you formerly walked according to the course of this world, according to the prince of the power of the air, of the spirit that is now working in the sons of disobedience. Among them we too all formerly lived in the lusts of our flesh, indulging the desires of the flesh

WHO IS GOD? WHO AM I?

and of the mind, and were by nature children of wrath, even as the rest. But God, being rich in mercy, because of His great love with which He loved us, even when we were dead in our transgressions, made us alive together with Christ (by grace you have been saved)." Verse 12 says, "remember that you were at that time separate from Christ, excluded from the commonwealth of Israel, and strangers to the covenants of promise, having no hope and without God in the world."

How are we separated from God and His kind of life? Underline five reasons above that tell how we are separated from God.

Do any of those five conditions apply to you? Why or why not?

_____
_____
_____

In the above scripture what is God willing to do for us?

_____
_____
_____

Read the next four verses.

Galatians 1:4— "… that He might rescue us from this present evil age…"

2 Peter 1:4— "… He has granted to us His precious and magnificent promises, so that by them you may become partakers of the divine nature, having escaped the corruption that is in the world by lust."

Isaiah 43:25— "I, even I, am the one who wipes out your transgressions for My own sake, and I will not remember your sins.

Romans 5:8-9— "But God demonstrates His own love toward us, in that while we were yet sinners, Christ died for us. Much more then, having now been justified by His blood, we shall be saved from the wrath of God through Him."

WHAT THE BIBLE SAYS ABOUT ETERNAL LIFE

Why do we need God's salvation and eternal life according to the above four verses?
___

In the above four verses, what does God do for us that makes it possible for us to have eternal life?
___

Romans 6:23 – "For the wages of sin is death, but the gift of God is eternal life in Christ Jesus our Lord."

According to Romans 6:23, does a person earn eternal life, or is it a gift from God?
___

When someone offers us a gift, when does it become ours?
___

In your own words, what would you say needs to happen to those who do not have a relationship with God?
___

What have you learned in this segment?
___

In the next segment we learn how to receive eternal life.

WHO IS GOD? WHO AM I?

SEGMENT THREE
HOW TO RECEIVE ETERNAL LIFE

John 6:66-69— "As a result of this many of His disciples withdrew and were not walking with Him anymore. So Jesus said to the twelve, 'You do not want to go away also, do you?' Simon Peter answered Him, 'Lord, to whom shall we go? You have words of eternal life. We have believed and have come to know that You are the Holy One of God.'"

Jesus asked his disciples if they wanted to go away from him. Why?

_____

_____

What was Peter's answer?

_____

_____

We all have the freedom of choice. What do you say? Do you want God's eternal life?

_____

_____

JESUS' WORDS ABOUT ETERNAL LIFE

John 3:14-16— "As Moses lifted up the serpent in the wilderness, even so must the Son of Man be lifted up; so that whoever believes will in Him have eternal life. For God so loved the world, that He gave His only begotten Son, that whoever believes in Him shall not perish, but have eternal life."

Who can have eternal life?

_____

_____

WHAT THE BIBLE SAYS ABOUT ETERNAL LIFE

How did Jesus make eternal life possible for us?

To what do the words "the Son of Man be lifted up" refer? (see segment two, Romans 5:8-9)

John 11:25-26—Jesus said to her, "I am the resurrection and the life; he who believes in Me will live even if he dies, and everyone who lives and believes in Me will never die. Do you believe this?" Notice what Jesus said to this woman. Notice his question to her. What is she being asked to believe?

TWO ILLUSTRATIONS OF WHAT IT MEANS TO BELIEVE IN JESUS

(1) A boat is at the dock of a lake. I believe the boat is real. I can see and touch it. I can believe all I want the truth that it is real, but that belief won't get me to the other side of the lake. I must get into the boat and let it take me where I want to go. Believing includes both; knowing it is real in my mind and committing my life to it by getting into the boat. So, it is with Jesus.

(2) A man is walking a tightrope across Niagara Falls. We watch him do it and we believe he can do it. We also watch him carry a person across. Wow, he is great, amazing. Then he asks to let him carry me across. Will I let him carry me? You would not trust just anybody, but believing in Jesus means you trust your life into His hands?

WHO IS GOD? WHO AM I?

Why or why not do you think you can trust Jesus to save you?

_____
_____
_____

COMMENT: Believing is not always easy. Believing in Jesus means (1) knowing he can do what he says and promises, and (2) letting him be in charge of my life by trusting him and committing my life into his care. Again, we see that eternal life is having a relationship with God. To have eternal life, as the next two scripture verses say, we must be in Him and He must be in us. We must become united with him as one.

John 14:20— "After a little while the world will no longer see Me, but you will see Me; because I live, you will live also. In that day you will know that I am in My Father, and you in Me, and I in you.

In this statement by Jesus, what does He promise his disciples?

_____
_____

What will they know?

_____
_____

John 17:22— "The glory which You have given Me I have given to them, that they may be one, just as We are one."

In this statement by Jesus, what has Jesus made possible for us?

_____
_____

In this segment, what have you have learned about how Jesus wants us to respond to his words of eternal life?

_____
_____
_____

WHAT THE BIBLE SAYS ABOUT ETERNAL LIFE

COMMENT: When we believe in Jesus, something happens to us. He comes to live in us and we in Him. When this happens mankind's fellowship was with God is restored. We are connected with God's eternal life once again. How can this be? How does our new birth happen?

We discover the answer in the next segment.

SEGMENT FOUR
GOD CAUSES US TO BE BORN INTO HIS FAMILY

John 1:10-13— "He was in the world, and the world was made through Him, and the world did not know Him. He came to His own, and those who were His own did not receive Him. But as many as received Him, to them He gave the right to become children of God, even to those who believe in His name, who were born, not of blood nor of the will of the flesh nor of the will of man, but of God."

What three things enable us to become God's children—what is our part and what is God's part?

_____
_____
_____
_____

COMMENT: To be born of Him means that, just as we are physically born into our human family, we can be spiritually born into God's family. To be born of Him means to be born by His Spirit. The Spirit in us is what enables us to have eternal life. "Receiving him" is like receiving a gift. What all is involved?

John 3:3-8—Jesus answered and said to him, "Truly, truly, I say to you, unless one is born again he cannot see the kingdom of God." Nicodemus said to Him, 'How can a man be born when he is old? He cannot enter a second time into his mother's womb and be born, can he?' Jesus answered, 'Truly, truly, I say to you, unless one is born of water and the Spirit he cannot enter into the kingdom of God. That which is born of the flesh is flesh, and that which is born of the Spirit is spirit. Do not be amazed that I said to you, you must be born again. The wind blows where it wishes and you hear the sound of it, but do not know where it comes from and where it is going; so is everyone who is born of the Spirit.'"

JESUS BAPTIZES US WITH HIS SPIRIT CAUSING US TO BE BORN OF GOD

Mark 1:8—John the Baptizer said: "I baptized you with water; but He will baptize you with the Holy Spirit."

Romans 8:9-11— "However, you are not in the flesh but in the Spirit, if indeed the Spirit of God dwells in you. But if anyone does not have the Spirit of Christ, he does not belong to Him. If Christ is in you, though the body is dead because of sin, yet the spirit is alive because of righteousness. But if the Spirit of Him who raised Jesus from the dead dwells in you, He who raised Christ Jesus from the dead will also give life to your mortal bodies through His Spirit who dwells in you."

COMMENT: Having God's Spirit living in us is what causes us to be born into God's family. God causes us to be born, by His Spirit, and His Spirit in us is what makes us to be one with God and Jesus.

Romans 10:13-15— "for 'WHOEVER WILL CALL ON THE NAME OF THE LORD WILL BE SAVED.' How then will they call on Him in whom they have not believed? How will they believe in Him whom they have not heard? And how will they hear without a preacher? How will they preach unless they are sent? Just as it is written, 'HOW BEAUTIFUL ARE THE FEET OF THOSE WHO BRING GOOD NEWS OF GOOD THINGS!'"

Ephesians 1:13— "In Him, you also, after listening to the message of truth, the gospel of your salvation—having also believed, you were sealed in Him with the Holy Spirit of promise…"

Galatians 3:2, 14— (verse 2) "This is the only thing I want to find out from you: did you receive the Spirit by the works of the Law, or by hearing with faith?" (verse 14) "in order that in Christ Jesus the blessing of Abraham might come to the Gentiles, so that we would receive the promise of the Spirit through faith."

WHAT THE BIBLE SAYS ABOUT ETERNAL LIFE

According to the verses above, when does the Holy Spirit and Jesus come into us?

_____
_____

Summarize what you have learned. What do you understand it means for you to be born of the Spirit?

_____
_____
_____
_____

Segment five answers: How can we know that Jesus lives in us and that we have eternal life?

SEGMENT FIVE
HOW WE KNOW WE HAVE ETERNAL LIFE

1 John 5:11-13 - And the testimony is this, that God has given us eternal life, and this life is in His Son. He who has the Son has the life; he who does not have the Son of God does not have the life. These things I have written to you who believe in the name of the Son of God, so that you may know that you have eternal life."

Why does John write this to believers?

_____
_____

Who has eternal life according to these verses?

_____
_____

WHO IS GOD? WHO AM I?

2 Corinthians 13:5— "Test yourselves to see if you are in the faith; examine yourselves! Or do you not recognize this about yourselves, that Jesus Christ is in you—unless indeed you fail the test?"

What are we asked to recognize about ourselves?

_____

_____

COMMENT: The next two passages tell us how we can test ourselves to know that Jesus is in us.

1 John 2:3-6— "By this we know that we have come to know Him, if we keep His commandments. The one who says, 'I have come to know Him,' and does not keep His commandments, is a liar, and the truth is not in him; but whoever keeps His word, in him the love of God has truly been perfected. By this we know that we are in Him: the one who says he abides in Him ought himself to walk in the same manner as He walked."

1 John 4:7-11— "Beloved, let us love one another, for love is from God; and everyone who loves is born of God and knows God. The one who does not love does not know God, for God is love. By this the love of God was manifested in us, that God has sent His only begotten Son into the world so that we might live through Him. In this is love, not that we loved God, but that He loved us and sent His Son to be the propitiation for our sins. Beloved, if God so loved us, we also ought to love one another."

In the previous two verses, what are two ways we know Jesus is living in us?

_____

_____

_____

_____

1 John 2:25, 29 – "This is the promise which He Himself made to us: eternal life." "If you know that He is righteous, you know that everyone also who practices righteousness is born of Him."

WHAT THE BIBLE SAYS ABOUT ETERNAL LIFE

According to this verse, how can we know that Jesus lives in us and we have eternal life?

_____

_____

(check out 1 Peter 1:3-9)

THE CONCLUSION OF THIS STUDY

God's chosen people, Israel, had hearts of stone. They kept going their own ways, prideful, ignorant of God's word, not wanting to hear it, stubborn, refusing to repent. They needed a new heart. God promised it. Ezekiel 36:26-27 says, "Moreover, I will give you a new heart and put a new spirit within you; and I will remove the heart of stone from your flesh and give you a heart of flesh. I will put My Spirit within you and cause you to walk in My statutes, and you will be careful to observe My ordinances." When we receive His promise by faith, God causes us to be born again. This new birth changes our heart so that we will love God and want to live His way. Genesis 2:7 says that when God breathed His breath of life into Adam, Adam became a living being. Likewise, when Jesus baptizes us with His Spirit, God breathes His life into us, and like Adam, we become a living being. We now have His eternal life in us. 1 John 4:13 says, "By this we know that we abide in Him and He in us, because He has given us of His Spirit." 2 Corinthians 5:17 says this, "Therefore if anyone is in Christ, he is a new creature; the old things passed away; behold, new things have come."

What about you? Who is God? Who are you? Do you have eternal life? How did you get it? How do you know you have it? Write your testimony here:

_____

_____

WHO IS GOD? WHO AM I?

WHO AM I? I HAVE ETERNAL LIFE. I AM NO LONGER WITHOUT GOD AND WITHOUT HOPE

I HAVE A NEW LIFE—John 5:24— "Truly, truly, I say to you, he who hears My word, and believes Him who sent Me, has eternal life, and does not come into judgment, but has passed out of death into life."

I HAVE A NEW RELATIONSHIP—Colossians 1:13-14—"For He rescued us from the domain of darkness and transferred us to the kingdom of His beloved Son, in whom we have redemption, the forgiveness of sins."

I HAVE A NEW FUTURE—John 14:1-3— "Do not let your heart be troubled; believe in God, believe also in Me. In My Father's house are many dwelling places; if it were not so, I would have told you; for I go to prepare a place for you. If I go and prepare a place for you, I will come again and receive you to Myself, that where I am, there you may be also."

I WILL HAVE A NEW BODY—Philippians 3:20-21— "For our citizenship is in heaven, from which also we eagerly wait for a Savior,

WHAT THE BIBLE SAYS ABOUT ETERNAL LIFE

the Lord Jesus Christ; who will transform the body of our humble state into conformity with the body of His glory, by the exertion of the power that He has even to subject all things to Himself."

IN THE NEXT CHAPTER we will discuss the subject of fear. Fear is a common problem for all humans. Be prepared, it is a long chapter mostly given to a study of the Biblical meaning of the "fear of the Lord." The chapter also includes human fears and how we overcome fear. "Do not fear" is an often-used phrase in the Bible.

Chapter 9

THE FEAR OF GOD AND OVERCOMING FEAR

AN INTRODUCTION

In times past there was a phrase often heard spoken that went something like this, "Somebody needs to put the fear of God into that person." What they meant was that the person referred to was behaving rather badly and the only thing that could change them would be "the fear of God." It is true! The fear of God does change people's bad attitudes and behaviors. The fear of God is still an important concept to be learned in any culture, and in any historical era, but especially in today's increasingly troubled world. Unfortunately, people know little about, or pay little attention, to "the fear of God." That is why the "fear of God" is a big part of the subject matter of this chapter. The Bible has a number of Hebrew and Greek words that are translated in our English Bibles as "fear." These Biblical words will enable us to learn what God wants us to know about fear as it relates to all aspects of your life and mine.

THE PLAN FOR THIS CHAPTER IS TO OBSERVE THREE BIBLICAL CATEGORIES OF FEAR

In reading the Bible we discover that it uses the words for "fear" in three ways: (1) The Bible frequently uses the phrase "the fear of God" or "the fear of the Lord;" (2) The Bible uses the word "fear" to refer to what we humans fear; and (3) The Bible uses the words "Fear not", or "Do not fear" to encourage us not to be afraid. We shall proceed with what the Bible says about each of these three categories of fear.

WHO IS GOD? WHO AM I?

CATEGORY (1)
WHAT DOES IT MEAN TO FEAR GOD?
WHY IS THE "FEAR OF GOD" IMPORTANT?

Here are a number of questions. The answer is the same for all of them. Guess what it is?

1. What causes persons to want to turn away from evil and live an upright life (Proverbs 3:7; 16:6; Job 1:1, 8)
2. What causes persons to desire and seek God's knowledge, wisdom, and understanding? (Proverbs 1:7; 9:10)
3. What causes persons to hate pride, arrogance, and a perverse mouth? (Proverbs 8:13)
4. What enables persons to live securely and be at ease from the dread of evil? (Proverbs 1:29-33)
5. What guards, protects, and delivers persons from devious people and the ways of evil? (Proverbs 2:5-15)
6. What enables persons to experience the blessings of God in their lives? (Psalm 112:1-6; Proverbs 19:23)
7. What leads persons to belief in God's salvation? (Exodus 14:30-31)
8. What does God want for all the inhabitants of the earth? (Psalm 33:8; Ecclesiastes 12:13)
9. What should believers in God and Jesus pray for? (Psalm 86:11)

TWO MEANINGS OF THE FEAR OF GOD

Pause to read Exodus 34:6-7. This passage, in whole or in part, is quoted often throughout scripture. [18] God tells us that He is both a loving God and a punishing God. God has a loving side to fear, and a punishing side to fear. When fear, often translated using the word "reverence." is used with the Lord God as its object, there are two

---

[18] (Check out: Numb. 14:18; Deut. 5:9-10; 7:9-10; Neh. 9:17; Psa. 86:5, 15; 103:7-14; 145:8-9; Jer. 9:23-26; 32:18; Joel 2:13; Jonah 4:2; Nahum 1:3; Rom. 2:4-5) A book worth reading that explains God's definition of Himself in Exodus 34:6-7 is John Mark Comer's, "God Has a Name" (Zondervan, Grand Rapids, MI, 2017).

aspects of God to fear, or revere. The first aspect sees God as a God of "terror." We can be terrified, scared, in dread of, or greatly intimidated by how God makes Himself known to us. We want to shy away, withdraw, or run from Him. The second aspect sees God as a God of love and compassion. We are attracted to His lovingkindness. This aspect of fear means we run toward God instead of running away from Him. God reveals Himself in ways that can bring about both elements of fear. Below, we explain in more detail the "terror" meaning of fear, followed by the compassionate meaning of fear.

THE TERROR MEANING OF FEARING GOD

There are four ways God appears as a terrifying or fearful God:

(1) God's presence can be terrifying. One example of God's terrifying presence occurs in the days of Moses, at a place called Mount Sinai. With thunder and lightning, God revealed Himself in an awesome and terrifying way (Read Exodus 19:16-25). After experiencing God's terrifying presence, the people did not want God to speak to them again. They told Moses, "Speak to us yourself and we will listen; but let not God speak to us, or we will die" Moses then said to the people, "Do not be afraid; for God has come in order to test you, and in order that the fear of Him may remain with you, so that you may not sin" (Read Exodus 20:18-20).

(2) God's wrath is terrifying. An example of God's terrifying wrath is when God appears unexpectedly to people who are not on God's side. They run for cover, fearing His wrath (Read Revelation 6:12-17). Here we see a "scared to death" fear of God felt by persons who have rejected God and have set aside His righteous ways of living (Proverbs 28:14; 2 Thessalonians 1:6-8). When we continue sinning against God by destroying what God intended to be good, we are in danger of finding ourselves in a place of no return (Proverbs 29:1). Jesus speaks of God's ultimate terror when he says concerning himself, "He who believes in the Son has eternal life; but he who does not obey the Son will not see life, but the wrath of God abides on him" (John 3:36). According to the Bible, it is a terrifying thing to live in the knowledge and expectation

of God's displeasure, judgment, and impending death (Read Hebrews 10:26-31).

(3) Being unsure of who God is can create fear. We don't know God well enough to know what to expect from Him. Jesus' disciples were in a life-threatening storm on a lake. Jesus was with them and spoke to the storm. The winds stopped and the raging life-threatening waves of water became calm. Jesus said to them, "Where is your faith? The disciples became very much afraid, saying, "Who then is this, that even the wind and the sea obey him?" They had not yet fully realized who Jesus was. (Read Mark 4:36-41). Another fearful experience occurred when Jesus appeared to his disciple after his resurrection from the dead. They were startled and frightened. (Read Luke 24:36-39). God's miraculous works can bring a strange kind of fear. We can fear things we do not understand, and lack of understanding often results in lack of trust.

(4) God's ultimate judgment of our lives can be terrifying (2 Corinthians 5:10-11). Knowing we've done wrong likely leads to fearing God's punishment. The apostle Peter, after fishing all night and catching nothing, was amazed by catching lots of fish at the command of Jesus. Peter felt terror-stricken in Jesus' presence, knowing he did not deserve God's goodness, but rather punishment for his unbelief and sinfulness. He fell down before Jesus and said, "Go away from me Lord, for I am a sinful man, O Lord" (Read Luke 5:4-8). Another example of the terrifying fear of God's punishment for sin was a part of the experience of the prophet Isaiah (Read Isaiah. 6:1-5). Let's now move to the second meaning of the fear of God.

THE COMPASSIONATE MEANING OF FEARING GOD

Because God is not only a God of justice in punishing wrongdoing, but is also a God of grace and mercy, there is the compassionate meaning of fear people can experience. Revering God will respect the terror side of God, but it also respects the other side of God—His goodness, mercy, compassion, forgiveness, and lovingkindness.

People who genuinely and reverently fear this side of God have decided they want God to be their God and to live His way. They are

UNDERSTANDING AND APPLYING

not being good and living right in order to avoid His punishment; rather, they are voluntarily being good and living right because they know God has loved, forgiven, and accepted them. Yes, there is always the knowledge of God's terrifying side, but that fear of God is alleviated and is overridden by a reverent attitude and love for God, one that is eager to obey and please Him. A reverent fear of God will cause a person to become like Him in one's holy, moral, and spiritual lifestyle (2 Corinthians 7:1; 1 Peter 1:14-16; 1 John 3:1-6).

God's love controls those who revere Him (2 Corinthians 5:14-15). Here is one Biblical example of what it means to have this loving reverent fear of God. God's people were slaves to the Egyptians, and the ruler of Egypt was afraid that the Israelites were getting too numerous and powerful for him to be able to control them. Therefore, the Pharoah ordered the Israelite midwives to kill all the Israelite boys at birth. Pharoah had no fear of God. But because those midwives feared God, they would not obey the king's orders to kill the babies. Fearing God meant that they would obey God by doing what was right as God wanted, not doing something wrong that the king wanted (Read Exodus 1:17-21). If this all seems confusing to you, keep reading and it may become clearer to you by the end.

BOTH SIDES OF THE FEAR OF GOD ARE TRUE

Many people see two differing God's in the Bible. The God of the Old Testament is the mean punishing God, and the God of the New Testament is the loving forgiving God. Actually, the Bible shows that God is the same in both the Old and New Testaments. When we understand the fear of God, both meanings of the word "fear" are true; He is loving all through the Bible and punishing all through the Bible. Understood properly, God's justice is also an act of love. We must learn to reverence God's terrorizing presence, and reverence God's lovingkindness. A proper fear of God is to revere God for who He is in His totality.

Read again Exodus 34:6-7. Being created in God's image, we humans have these same traits in us. Like God, we are compassionate and loving on the one hand and concerned for justice and punishment

WHO IS GOD? WHO AM I?

of the wicked on the other. We have a sense of love and mercy toward people who are suffering and needing help. We want to help them. We also have anger toward people who hurt others, and we want justice to be done. Isn't it strange how we think it is okay for us to have both sides to our human nature, but when it comes to God, we only want a God of love, and we reject a God of justice and punishment. Here is an interesting story I once heard. A man gave a talk on God's moral standards which included both love and punishing the guilty. Afterward, a woman argued with him saying, "There are no absolute truths or absolute moral standards in the world that we can trust. Therefore, we must make our own truth and standards of what is right or wrong. She chose to believe in loving people over judging and punishing. To show that there are standards of moral right and wrong within all of us, the man listening to her grabbed her phone, put it in his pocket, and began to walk away. "Wait", she objected, "that's my phone, are you going to give it back?" "No" he responded, "why should I?" "Because it's wrong", she said. "I thought you just told me that we all need to set our own standards of moral right and wrong. My moral standard is that if I need something and someone has what I need, it is alright for me to help myself to it." She became angry. It's easy to believe only in a God of love until we become the victim of evil doing. All of a sudden, justice seems important.

DOES THE FEAR OF GOD LEAD TO SALVATION?

<u>Can a terror of God lead to God's salvation?</u> Yes, if one yields to God and trusts one's life into God's care (Exodus 14:30-31). Being confronted with the terrifying side of God, can be a necessary experience leading to salvation and the loving reverence of God. For those who respond to God's revelation of terror, not by rejecting God, but by moving toward God, such a fear of God will cause one to yield to God. In yielding to God, the person will come to see His compassionate, loving, and forgiving side. This discovered knowledge of God's lovingkindness and salvation, coming out of a fear of God's terrible power and awesomeness, leads to a reverence toward God that will eventually overcome one's fear of God's terrible side. Joshua 2:1-

UNDERSTANDING AND APPLYING

21 is a good example of being saved due to a terrifying fear of God. Check it out. What do you think?

Proverbs 17:11 says "A rebellious man seeks only evil." Those who rebel against God by rejecting His revelation will not yield to God. But those who believe in God, because of His terrifying revelation, are ones who have chosen to fear God. Their fear of God leads to belief in a saving God and results in God's blessing and new life (Hebrews 11:6). The terrifying role of God in revealing Himself has a part to play in a person's salvation.

<u>Can reverence for God's compassion lead to God's salvation?</u> Yes, according to Romans 2:4-5. However, there are people who reverently fear God and who do good in the sight of God, but they are not yet saved as defined in the Bible. They are God-fearing people who are not against God, nor are they scared of God. They may be thinking that believing in God and doing their best to live as God wants is what saves them, but God has a message for those who believe in Him and are not yet saved. When an unsaved person who fears God, hears and believes the message of God's good news, he or she gladly accepts it and is saved from sin and death (John 3:16; Ephesians 1:13-14). An example of this is a man named Cornelius who feared God but was yet unsaved. (Read Acts 10 & 11). When Peter met him, Peter said: "I most certainly understand now that God is not one to show partiality, but in every nation the man who fears Him and does what is right is welcome to Him" (Acts 10:34-35). When Peter told Cornelius God's message, Cornelius believed and received God's Spirit. God gives His Spirit to people who believe so they acquire a new heart, bear his divine nature within them, and grow to become like God (Ezekiel 36:24-28; 1 Peter 1:1-11).

REVERENCING THE CONSUMING FIRE AND TERROR SIDE OF GOD

How can we respect and reverence God as a consuming fire who judges the guilty and puts people to death? Like others, I struggle with some of God's actions. I may cringe, and I do cringe when I read in the Bible some of the things God does. But going deeper to understand God

WHO IS GOD? WHO AM I?

helps me to reverence the terror side of God. God's nature and actions make more sense to me if I am open to give serious consideration to the following truths about God.

(1) God does not want anyone to die; but for all to repent, place their trust in Him, and receive His gift of eternal life. His heart is grieved concerning the wickedness He sees in His created world, and God mourns for people who are suffering from the evils of the world that are both in and around them. I understand more of the heart of God when I read Genesis 6:5-6; Luke 19:41-44; Ezekiel 18:23, 32; Jeremiah 8:18-22; and John 3:16.

(2) God is patient and does all He can to give persons the opportunity to accept Him, be changed, and live by His righteous ways (2 Peter 3:9). God gave 400 years for the Amorite, Canaan's people, to repent of their iniquities (Genesis 15:16). He also offers to provide everything a person needs to be changed, experience a new life, and be remade into the image of God-likeness (Isaiah 55:1-3, 7; John 7:37-39).

(3) God's judgments are perfectly fair and just. Because He knows all the facts, God is the only one with the capability and the right to ultimately judge the world, and all of us. Abraham, the father of our faith, believed this about God. He pleaded with God to save his nephew from dying in an act of God's judgment. He said, "Will you indeed sweep away the righteous with the wicked? Far be it from You to do such a thing…Shall not the judge of all the earth deal justly (Genesis 18:23-25)? Also, God does more than punish people for their wrongs; He also rewards people for their good (Revelation 22:12).

(4) God is an all-consuming fire so as to eliminate all wickedness and evil. Check out some of God's plans: Acts 17:30-31; Psalm 9:8; 96:11-13; Isaiah 65:17; 66:15-16; 2 Thessalonians 1:5-9; Revelation 20:12; 2 Corinthians 5:10. What enables a new world of goodness, peace, and righteousness to exist and be newly created? The truth is, a God of love will destroy the evils that are ruining people's lives and His created world. A person's fear of God, due to reading about His judgments, may create terror. However, if we understand God's purpose and plan to restore all things (Acts 3:17-21), such knowledge may lead to a personal peace with God.

UNDERSTANDING AND APPLYING
HOW WE CAN REVERENCE A TERRIFYING GOD WITHOUT BEING TERRIFIED

When God shows the terrifying side of Himself it demonstrates His awesome power. This can cause people to run from Him. But to reverence His power causes us who believe in Him to run toward Him when we realize that God is our rock, our shield, our strength, and our defender. God is a strong and powerful God who is able to protect me. His power is a guarantee to me that nothing is able to stop Him from fulfilling His promises to bring me into a good and evil free world. No more sin, pain, suffering, and death. He is a warrior God who fights for me to bring me to His safe and peaceful place, my future home. I can trust Him to do so because I know His awesome power is greater than any other power that exists. While God's powerful displays can put a terrifying fear in people, for me, I am able to reverence that same terrifying power as a power showing me that God is able to protect and save me. Therefore, I have a reverential fear of God's terrifying side. Yes, it is a power that can destroy those who will not believe, and who continue in their wicked ways, but it is a power that can save all true believers from all the evil powers in this world that rise up and threaten to destroy them. As the Bible says, "The name of the LORD is a strong tower; the righteous runs into it and is safe (Proverbs 18:10). Revealing His awesome and terrifying power is for me a sign of God's love for all who are on His side. If you want to read the great good news of how this terrifying God uses His power to destroy the wickedness of this world and bring those who are righteous into His new world, read Isaiah 65:1-25. It will totally cause you who are righteous to fear God by reverencing His terrifying and awesome power. I use the word "righteous" for people who are saved by God because in both the Old and New Testaments of the Bible, those who believe God's message of grace and salvation are declared by God to be righteous (Genesis 15:1-6; Philippians 3:7-9).

Some will object that God does not protect people from the many storms of nature that afflict us all. If these are acts of God, they often kill the righteous along with the unrighteous. How then, can we say that God's power shields and protects us? It is true that the righteous

WHO IS GOD? WHO AM I?

followers of God and Jesus can be killed in this world by a corrupted earth, and also by wicked people who murder many who are innocent. Death in this world of sin is real. The fact is, however, that God does often protect people from the threats of death encountered in this world. Many live through them to tell of God's mercy and sometimes miraculous help to save them. My wife and I have each experienced God's help in the face of hardships and potential death. We believers are called to trust God's goodness, even in the face of afflictions or death. Suffering is never something we enjoy going through, but praying and trusting God for help is easier to do if we know who God is and who we are. I offer the following scriptures that address this objection that God is not always protective of his beloved people. Read Psalm 66. The Psalm writer encourages us to praise God and trust His lovingkindness in spite of troubles. Read Proverbs 10: 2, 16, 24, and 28-30. These verses show us what the righteous can expect from the God who is for them. Let these verses lift your spirits. Even though they may not always come true in this world, there is a time they will come true. To be assured of this, review again Isaiah 65, God's words of hope that will never fail. One more scripture to consider is the way we are to live in the midst of trials and tribulations. Read John 9:1-41. It's the story of a blind man whom Jesus healed. Jesus went about doing good, using the miraculous and awesome power of God to rescue people. We are to live as Jesus lived, going about doing good in an evil world. The Bible says doing good overcomes evil (Romans 12:21). In Jesus' life there were people against him who eventually were successful in killing him on a cross. What is important for us to know is that Jesus did not stay dead. For all of those who come to Jesus and receive his salvation, the same is true. We never die and will one day be bodily raised from the dead just as Jesus was. We love as he loved and we never stop doing good, for death can never destroy us. Whether our body dies when we are young, or old, God's awesome power gives us a hope that will come true, a hope that enables us to endure and overcome hardships, and death itself.

UNDERSTANDING AND APPLYING
MOVING BEYOND THE FEAR OF GOD'S PUNISHMENT TO BEING AT PEACE WITH GOD

All is not doom and gloom with God. Yes, God is a God of righteous justice who must destroy evil for the sake of restoring a good world, but God is also love, and His love is patient, merciful and forgiving. When we experience God's loving forgiveness and acceptance, we no longer have to fear punishment for our wrongs. Jesus took God's punishment for us. Because of God's love for us, and our love for Him, His love casts out the fear of punishment (I John 4:16-18). This reverent fear of God changes our lives so that we are made one in heart with the heart of God. We want to do God's will and live by His standards of righteousness. God knows that sin and evil is inevitable in a world of created free-will beings. Happily, people can be forgiven their wrongs, be reconciled to Him, and enjoy peace with God (Romans 5:1).

Still, there are some reasons people may not enjoy peace with God. Christian people, when they go through hard times, may wonder, "Is God punishing me for something I did wrong?" It is especially easy to feel this way if they know they are not living as God wants, or if Satan brings their past sins to mind. During hard times it is okay if we feel that God has abandoned us, even Jesus temporarily felt that way. But if you think that God is punishing you, and you fear facing God's judgment, the following points may help you find peace with God. We all need to know we are at peace with God. But how can we know?

PROBLEMS PREVENTING PEACE WITH GOD.

Following are seven reasons that affect our peace with God. Honestly recognizing what is preventing our peace with God can help us to overcome our fears. Think for a moment of how the seven problems below can destroy one's peace with God. Which ones are true of you? Is there any other problem you can name?

(1) Rejection of God: I can't believe in a mean God who is angry, wrathful, and kills people.

WHO IS GOD? WHO AM I?

(2) Fear: I know days of judgment are coming and I fear facing God (2 Corinthians 5:9-10).

(3) Abandonment: God seems distant. He doesn't answer my prayers. I feel He doesn't care about me.

(4) Questioning: Bad things are happening to me. Is God punishing me for something I've done wrong?

(5) Hopelessness: God can't love and want me; I've done too many really bad things in my life.

(6) Ignorance: I wasn't raised in a religious family and don't know the Bible very well (Ephesians 4:17-19).

(7) Doubt/Skepticism: My mind and experiences tell me not to believe God's word (Matthew 14:28-31).

FACTS THAT MAY HELP US OVERCOME A LACK OF PEACE WITH GOD.

(1) Check to make sure you are a true Christian. According to the Bible, what are the characteristics of a saved person? Have you heard and understood the meaning of Jesus' death on the cross, that he died to pay for your sins so that you can be forgiven by God? Have you confessed your need for Jesus, received and believed that he came into your life to transform you into a new person? Do you know that his Holy Spirit lives in you? 2 Corinthians 13:5 says to test and examine yourself to see if Christ is in you. As far as you know, are you in good standing with God? Peace with God comes when you are justified (Romans 5:1-2).

(2) Honestly observe your heart's attitude toward God. What kind of relationship do you have and want with God? Do you have a heart that desires to love and serve God (Deuteronomy 5:29)? Do you find yourself living by God's word and the Lord's teachings (1 John 2:1-6)? Peace is knowing you are trying to do so.

(3) Believe what the Bible says about who you are in Christ. Knowing and believing who God says you are gives assurance of peace with God. Underline who God says you are in Ephesians, chapters 1 and 2?

UNDERSTANDING AND APPLYING

(4) Doubting the Bible can hinder peace with God. Why do you believe the Bible is the word of God? What evidences convince you beyond reasonable doubt that the Bible is true? It is your choice to believe or not.

(5) When you read the Bible and notice that God is angry and punishes the guilty, ask yourself, what is the Bible's description of the one's being punished? Who are the wicked; how are they described? Read Joshua 23:16; Romans 1:28-32; Galatians 5:19-21; and 2 Timothy 3:1-5. Then compare them with who you are. Are you wicked like them? If the answer is "No", then God is not going to treat you the same as those whose wickedness is destroying the people and culture around them. You are His child, and He loves you (1 John 3:1-3).

(6) Sometimes you may feel that God is punishing you. You must distinguish between God's punishment and God's discipline. God disciplines His people whom He loves so that they may share His holiness (read Hebrews 12:3-11).

(7) Do you know God well enough to trust Him and know He is with you and for you (Romans 8:31-39)? Recall how God has shown you that He cares for you in daily life? I have written in a journal about all the experiences I can remember of how God has shown He cares for me. Here is one example. Neighborhood kids were playing in the front yard at my house. I was sitting on my bike under a huge tree. My dog was continually barking on the enclosed front porch of my house. Finally, I got tired of hearing the barking and went to open the porch door to let her out. As soon as I touched the door handle, I heard a loud crash behind me. A large branch from the tree I was under broke off and had fallen on top of the bike where I was sitting. Luck, or God? One other example. We were moving from Montana to the Detroit area of Michigan. We needed a GPS to help us know how to get around in an unknown area. We had one but lost the cord to plug it in to the car. We were on our way out the door to leave when a friend stopped by to say goodbye and give us a gift. Having no idea that we had a GPS with a lost cord, the gift was a GPS exactly like the one we had, with the cord we needed. Luck, or God? You may be able to recall things like this that have happened in your life. These are events that some would call chance. I choose to believe, as some would say, "someone upstairs

must have been looking out for you." If there are times when I feel God is upset with me, or has abandoned me, I think of my journal and am reminded that God does care for me. He is with me and for me all the time (1 Peter. 5:7).

(8) Do you believe the love that God has for you? Knowing He loves you gives you peace by taking away the fear of punishment (1 John 4:16-18).

(9) God tests hearts (Proverbs 17:3; 21:2; Psalm 17:3). How? One way is through problems that come into our lives. Another is through commands He gives us to see if we will obey them. Abraham is the father of our faith (Galatians 3:6-9). If you study His life you will see that there were times, he struggled to believe God was with Him. But those times of testing taught him not to fear, but to trust God. It is in our struggles that our trust in God matures. In the end, Abraham shows mature faith when God told him to sacrifice the son God had promised him. He trusted God completely, believing that even if he killed him, God would raise him back to life (Hebrews 11:17-19). Jesus' disciples also struggled with trusting. When fear controlled them, Jesus asked, "Where is your faith?" (Luke 8:22-25). They did not know Jesus well enough to trust him. Do you?

DOING YOUR OWN STUDY OF WHAT THE BIBLE SAYS ABOUT "THE FEAR OF GOD"

By studying "fear of God" passages in the Bible, the goal is to learn more about who God is and who you are. Ask God to open your eyes and give insight as you read and study. Each time you read a verse in the Bible that has to do with fearing God you can choose from among the following questions to help you gain deeper insights. It may be that not every question will apply to each passage. Asking questions is a good way to learn about the fear of God from a study of the Bible. Here are the questions that can help you in your study. PAUSE: Short study: Apply questions to Proverbs 23:17-18. Long study: Look up Jeremiah 32:36-42. This passage is about the city of Jerusalem that was destroyed and its people taken captive to Babylon. Use the questions by doing a little study of your own to learn what it says about the fear of the Lord.

UNDERSTANDING AND APPLYING

1. Who are the characters involved in this passage? What is said about each of the characters involved?
2. What does the fear of the Lord mean in this situation, or verse?
3. How does the fear of the Lord affect the life of the person, or persons, who fear God?
4. How is life affected for those who choose not to fear God?
5. Who does God desire to fear Him? Why would God want people to fear Him?
6. Does this passage tell how God instills His fear into people?
7. Does God test people to see if they fear Him or not? What is the test?
8. Do any questions come to your mind? How can you find an answer?

I will now share a few things I have learned about the fear of God from my own study. You may agree or not, which is why doing your own study is important. I pray that as I share what I've discovered about the meaning of the "fear of God," you will better understand God, and who you are in fellowship with God.

FEARING GOD BEGINS WITH GOD MAKING HIMSELF KNOWN

When reading God's word, it becomes obvious that there are many ways God can make Himself known. He can make Himself known through a visible act that demonstrates His awesomeness and power, through a vision or dream, or through a physical appearance in some form of His choosing, even a human form. God can speak to us through an audible voice, or a voice heard in our mind. God can reveal Himself through an answer to a prayer, through an angel, through nature as we study it more closely, or through other people sharing with us what God has done for them. God reveals Himself through His Son Jesus who we read about in God's written book, or who may appear in person to someone, as he did to Paul. He could speak through a storm as He did with Martin Luther. He could speak through thunder and lightning on a mountain, or fire in a bush, or the voice of a donkey, or life's unexplainable circumstances. It is likely that because we are created in God's image, a basic belief built into our conscience tells us there is a

WHO IS GOD? WHO AM I?

God to whom we are responsible. In some way, God makes Himself known to us so that we can become aware of His existence, become open to information about Him, and to want to learn what He is like. A relationship with God, or a non-relationship, begins when we recognize that God has done something to make Himself known. The fact that He makes Himself known gives us an opportunity to respond to Him.

FEARING GOD MUST HAVE A PERSONAL BEGINNING

Stop and think about it. Is there a time in your life when you first became aware of the existence of the God of the Bible. How did it impact you? Here is a personal example. I remember one of my first real encounters with God. As a young boy I folded a sheet of paper to make an airplane. Every time I threw it the paper fell to the ground. For some reason, I said a prayer to God to help my airplane fly. The next time I threw it; the plane sailed beautifully across the room. I remember thinking, "Wow, God is real." Has He convincingly shown Himself real at times throughout your life. How or when did you consciously become aware of the Biblical God; or even if there is a God, or gods?

Certainly, the God or gods whom each of us believes in will have a lot to do with the culture and the family in which we were raised. We learn about God from them. For our purposes at present, we will not get off on the variety of "gods" and the various religions in this world. We must stay focusing on the God who is presented in His book called the Bible. How and when do individuals come to have a belief in the existence of that God? Maybe you can't recall such a time. Maybe you feel as if you have always believed there was a God. Maybe being created in God's image means that a belief in God is a basic belief within each one of us. Nevertheless, we can't have a proper fear of God if we are not aware of the existence of the God we are to fear. We will not be drawn to God unless we believe that He is and that He is a rewarder of those who seek Him. (Again, I refer to Hebrews 11:6) Once there is this awareness, a person is now open, or has a reason, or a curiosity, or a desire, to find out who is this God. Then, as your knowledge about God increases, and your attitudes become favorable toward Him, you will find yourself accepting God's input into your life and also being rewarded for a faith that seeks Him. Following are specific statements of what fearing God involves for those seeking Him.

FEARING GOD IS THE BEGINNING OF KNOWLEDGE, WISDOM, AND UNDERSTANDING

Proverbs 1:7 says, "The fear of the LORD is the beginning of knowledge; Fools despise wisdom and instruction." Proverbs 9:10 says, "The fear of the LORD is the beginning of wisdom, and the knowledge of the Holy One is understanding." The book of Proverbs tells us that the fear of the Lord is what starts you and me on a path of learning to know God, His wisdom, and His understanding. God's wisdom, understanding, and how to live life is worth more than all the money and wealth that this world could possibly give us. Nothing you or I could ever want compares to the value of possessing God's wisdom. Take a moment to read the following Proverbs to help you realize the value of wisdom, and some of the benefits it adds to your life: (Read Proverbs 1:5; 2:2-11; 3:13-26; 4:5-13; 8:11-17, and 8:32-36).

Notice that Proverbs 8:32 is a warning to those who hate God's wisdom and refuse to live by it. Proverbs 1:7 says, "fools despise wisdom and instruction." Proverbs 1:22 says, "How long, O naive ones, will you love being simple-minded? And scoffers delight themselves in scoffing and fools hate knowledge?" God has a word for the foolish person, pleading with them to fear Him and warning them of the consequences of rejecting Him and not accepting His knowledge. God says to them,

> Turn to my reproof, Behold, I will pour out my spirit on you; I will make my words known to you. Because I called and you refused, I stretched out my hand and no one paid attention; and you neglected all my counsel and did not want my reproof; I will also laugh at your calamity; I will mock when your dread comes, When your dread comes like a storm

and your calamity comes like a whirlwind, when distress and anguish come upon you, then they will call on me, but I will not answer; they will seek me diligently but they will not find me, because they hated knowledge and did not choose the fear of the LORD. They would not accept my counsel; they spurned all my reproof. So they shall eat of the fruit of their own way and be satiated with their own devices (Proverbs 1:23-31).

These words certainly explain why a person is a fool to reject God's input into their lives. I'm sure people reject God for various reasons. In their minds they have valid reasons. But, even so, God loves them and extends an invitation to them in Proverbs 9:4-6. Woe to those described in Romans 1:18-32.

FEARING GOD IS SOMETHING THAT CAN BE LEARNED

A primary way we learn to fear the Lord is by reading His words found in His book, the Bible. The king of Israel was to learn to fear the Lord by reading God's word (Deuteronomy 17:18-20). The people were to learn to fear the Lord in the same way (Deuteronomy 31:11-13). How does God motivate people to fear and learn of Him? Here are some ways: God motivates by acts of terror which people experience (Exodus 14:30-31), by hearing from others the terrifying things God can or will do (Jonah 3:3-10), or by acts of God's kindness which people experience (Acts 14:15-17; Romans 2:4). There are two primary motivations for things we do in this life—fear and love. We will want to learn the meaning of "the fear of the Lord" when God initiates within us the desire to do so. As we grow in our understanding of God, His word, and His lovingkindness, our reverence for Him deepens, and our lives are transformed toward being, once again, like God, displaying His image in us. When a person truly fears the Lord, it is the beginning of a lifetime of wanting to keep learning. God's Son, Jesus, invites us to come to him and learn from him (Matthew 11:28-30).

UNDERSTANDING AND APPLYING
FEARING GOD IS A CHOICE.

Notice what Proverbs 1:29 says about the foolish person who does not fear the Lord; "they did not choose to fear the Lord." You and I have a choice to make. Also, according to Joshua 22:25, it's possible to choose to stop fearing the Lord. As we continue learning more about God, we will develop beliefs about Him and attitudes toward Him. As we've learned thus far, God tells us clearly who He is. What He reveals, and how He reveals it, and how much we know Him, will determine the kind of fear we will have toward Him. Is He a terrifying God, or a loving God? Will we reject God or move toward God? Will we choose not to fear Him, or to fear Him? Joshua, a leader of Israel, told the people to choose whom they would serve. Thy could choose to serve their false gods, or the Lord who clearly made Himself known to them (Joshua 24:14-20). We also have a choice. We can choose to fear God or not. God has made Himself knowable to us earthlings in many ways. How we have perceived God can cause us to move away from God or to move toward Him. We can believe there is a God or choose to be our own god. Read the apostle Paul's speech in Acts 17:26-34. What choice do those from every nation have who hear about God?

Again, I refer to this Biblical story (Joshua 2) of people who chose to fear God, and those who chose not to fear God. Notice the "rewards," that is, the consequences of their choice. There was a woman not from God's chosen people, Israel. She and her nation heard about Israel's God from reports they received about God's parting of the Red Sea, thus saving His people from their enemies. Also, they knew of God's destruction of two wicked nations living across the river from them. This woman, and her people from the surrounding countryside, heard the same news of God's power and His saving of the Israelites. They all knew that Israel's God was greater than any gods they had worshipped. Certainly, Israel's God was worthy of their faith and commitment. When the opportunity came to side with God over their own gods, the surrounding people of her own culture rejected God, while this woman chose to fear God and join with God's people. Even though the rest of her people were afraid of Israel and their God, they chose not to fear God as she did. Her fear of God and her faith in Him was rewarded, for her life and the lives of her family members was saved. Those who chose not to fear God as she did, perished. Read about Rahab and her reverence toward God in Joshua 2:1-14 and in Hebrews 11:31.

FEARING GOD IS TO PRACTICE GOD'S STANDARDS OF RIGHT AND WRONG

Fearing God means you believe there is a God who deserves to be revered and obeyed. Fearing God means to choose to please God, doing as God wants, even if others want you to do something else. It means you are learning from God what is right and wrong. Job 1:1; 2:3 says that Job was an upright man, "fearing God and turning away from evil." Fearing God determines our moral standards. We will do good and not evil. Fearing God is to become holy as God is holy (Numbers 15:27-31; Leviticus 19:2; Matthew 5:48; 2 Corinthians 7:1). Our aim is to purify ourselves and not continue to sin. You can use the scriptures in this paragraph, along with the following, for a Bible study and discussion: (Deuteronomy 30:11-20; Romans 6:1-14; Hebrews 12:4-11; 1 John 2:1-6; 3:2-10). The fear of God by the midwives in Exodus 1:17-21 (already mentioned in this book) is an example of this. Reverence toward God, rightly understood and practiced, is the cause of all we do; it is the controlling factor of our whole life. When I was a young boy, my mom told me to clean up the living room. I threw a few things behind the couch, thinking no one would know. In that moment, the thought came to me, "God knows." I retrieved the items and put them away properly. I feared God.

FEARING GOD CAN PROTECT US FROM PEOPLE WHO DO NOT FEAR GOD.

If we know that a person fears God, we can expect them to treat us in a kind or civil way so that we do not need to fear them. If we come across people who do not fear God, it can make us afraid of people because they have no knowledge of God's moral standards of right and wrong. Read about Abraham and Sarah (Genesis 20:1-11). Read about Lot and Sodom (Genesis 19:1-16). What was Lot's concern when

UNDERSTANDING AND APPLYING

visitors came to town? How do we know Lot feared God? How did God protect Lot from those who did not fear God?

FEARING GOD IS WHAT BRINGS GOD'S BLESSINGS AND REWARDS INTO OUR LIVES

The God-fearing person can expect that all of God's benefits and promises to him or her will be fulfilled and enjoyed. The God-fearing person who has been declared righteous by God can look forward to inheriting a new world created by God (Romans 4:13; Matthew 5:5; Revelation 21:4-7). Proverbs 19:23 tells us one of God's blessings for fearing Him, "The fear of the LORD leads to life, so that one may sleep satisfied, untouched by evil." Such a blessing means that we have overcome our fears of evil. There are other rewards that come out of revering God. You will be blessed as you continue to learn more about the meaning of the fear of God. Study Proverbs 1:7; 2:4-5; 1:20-33; 3:7; 10:27; 14:2, 26-27; 15:16; 16:6; 22:4; 23:17-18; 28:14; 31:30; Ecclesiastes 3:12-14; 8:12-13; 12:13-14) What are the most important things to learn from these verses? Doing your own study about "fear of God" verses and passages involving stories, as mentioned earlier, can bring more blessings and rewards into your life. And remember, our goal is not just more knowledge about God, but to know God and have a close friendship.

We are now ready to move on to the final two categories of the word "fear" as used in the Bible. Some have said there are 365 times in the Bible where God says not to fear, one for every day of the year. I fact-checked this and found one person who listed all the verses in the Bible where it says, "do not fear" or its equivalence, and there were less than 160. That is still lots. To enjoy a mature faith in God, and experience His peace, God would have us replace fear with trust.

CATEGORY (2)
WHAT ARE WE HUMANS AFRAID OF?

When you think of the word "fear," what comes to mind? A life-threatening illness, a financial loss, panic attacks, spiders, or riding in

WHO IS GOD? WHO AM I?

airplanes? Maybe you worry about family problems, or problems at work. Maybe you are scared of the dark, or of being alone. Maybe you are dreading the future; what you must face tomorrow, or world-wide threats such as war or the world's end. There is seemingly no end to the number of things humans fear. Fear is a common experience among all humans, and it has many causes.

The Bible tells stories about real life, and like us, the Bible's characters often experience fear. We have all experienced similar fears throughout the years of our lives. Here are nine common fears the Bible emphasizes, followed by Biblical references to check out. We fear what other people may do to us (Genesis 50:18-21; Acts 18:9-10; Hebrews 13:6). We fear death (Genesis 21:16-17; Hebrews 2:15). We fear nature's harmful disasters, such as storms and diseases (Psalm 46:2-3; Mark 4:37-39; Acts 27:14-17). We fear that our daily needs may not be met (Matthew 6:25, 34). We fear what might happen in the future (Luke 21:25-26). We fear leaving our comfort zone and facing threatening situations (1 Samuel 17:23-24, 32). We fear admitting the truth about ourselves (Proverbs 28:13; John 3:19-20). We fear authorities and getting caught for things we've done wrong (Romans 13:3-4). We fear God's judgment and punishment for our wrongs (Genesis 3:10; 1 John 4:18). As you read through the Bible, you will find examples of these, and other things that people fear.

TWO SIDES OF FEAR

Fear has a positive and a negative side, perhaps both operating at the same time. Fear can cause us to run from something threatening to a place of safety. Fear can act as a warning of danger, triggering in our body the strength we need to overcome it, whether to run or fight. Fear can cause us to freeze up, to become motionless and unable to respond as we ought. Fear can lead to being timid or cowardly, failing to bravely handle the situation as needed. Fear can prevent us from pursuing our dreams and wishes, or from engaging in good things of everyday life that God means for us to enjoy. We experience lots of fears. Fear inspires caution and alerts us to things we need to be concerned about. We need to admit our fears and ask ourselves, "Why am I afraid?" and

UNDERSTANDING AND APPLYING

"What do I need to do about it?" Jesus once asked his disciples, "Why are you afraid?" Then, he made them think about the cause (Mark 4:40). Fear can be good and bad.

A WAY TO VIEW HUMAN EMOTIONS IN GENERAL

I like to view emotions as thermostats. Thermostats let us know how things are, for example, a furnace thermostat tells us if the temperature in the room is cold or hot. Then, if needed, we can make a necessary adjustment. Like a thermostat, emotions tell us that something is good or that something is not so good. Because emotions can appear suddenly, we may not be able to evaluate our emotions at the moment. Nevertheless, at an opportune time, it might be good to stop and think about whether the emotion is good or not, and whether or not an adjustment is needed. Anytime we experience an emotion, whether fear, jealousy, anger, joy, pride, and so forth, we may need, at some point, to ask ourselves, "Why am I feeling this way? Emotions are not necessarily wrong; they just happen. But too often we let our feelings control our lives instead of us controlling them. Letting our emotions control us can create harmful consequences. Understanding what is causing our emotion can help us to not let emotions dictate how we live. Emotions can be confusing. There can be a good reason for a negative emotion, or there may be a bad reason for a good emotion. It's healthy to look within ourselves and honestly analyze our emotions, even to have another help us if we feel unable or too confused to do so.

You are probably familiar with Biblical story involving Cain and Abel. The story gives us an example of how important it is to rightly handle our emotions. In Genesis 4:3-15, a man named Cain was angry at his brother. God asked Cain why he was angry? Asking "why," and coming to a correct conclusion, can be a powerful way to gain self-control and achieve what is good and right. God said to Cain about his anger, "you must master it." Did Cain do what God said? No, he did not. What resulted was that Cain killed his brother. Our emotions will get us into trouble if we let them wrongfully control our behavior. In other words, we must learn to master our emotions rather than let them control us, and we need God's help in doing so. Knowing God and His truth must be part of our consideration when trying to determine what is right or wrong and what to do. We move now to the third category of fear; do not fear, or fear not.

CATEGORY (3)
DO NOT FEAR

It is interesting to me that the Bible says God is to be feared, but at the same time it says not to fear? How do we get over the improper fears that we experience in normal daily living? Following, I share some things about my life of fear and how God has helped me, and is helping me, to deal with it.

HOW TO OVERCOME FEAR

I have been a fearful person almost all of my life. I have often said that my favorite character in the Bible is Gideon. I could identify with Gideon because, like me, he was afraid of many things. If you read Judges 6-8 you will see how fearful Gideon is and how God helps him overcome his fears. For some reason, I grew up being fearful. I was very shy and withdrawn. If I saw someone coming toward me on the sidewalk, I would cross the street to avoid them. My fears include the following. Coming home, I would go through the house to make sure no one was there. In bed at night, If I heard a noise, my body froze. I could not move to check it out. As a kid, if my friends rode their bikes down a dangerous looking steep hill, I would not do it. As an adult, I was scared of flying in airplanes. In school, I feared having to answer questions. In college, I avoided classes if I thought I would have to speak in front of the class. One night, when I was around 12 years old, I had a panic attack because I was afraid of dying. My mother came into my room to see why I was crying. She told me the best news I ever heard. She told me what Jesus said, "He who believes in me will never die." I believed it and from then on, I've been relying on God's help to overcome my fears. My journey from being a very fear-filled person in the past, to the victories over fear that I experience today, has been a slow and step-by-step process. With God's help, I have come a long

UNDERSTANDING AND APPLYING

way in not being afraid. We all differ. Some have little problem with fear in their lives, while others struggle with fears, worries, and anxieties. Following are ways God is using to help me to overcome fear. Perhaps some of them you have also learned, and if not, my sharing them may help you.

(1) MEMORIZE A BRIEF PORTION OF SCRIPTURE. I have chosen to memorize Psalm 23:1-6. I began by reading a verse and then trying to say it without looking. Once I knew it, I added another verse until I had it all memorized. As I lay in bed before falling asleep, or if I awaken in the night, I repeat the whole Psalm, or part of it, and I often focus my thoughts on a word or phrase. For example, I may think about what it means for Jesus to be my shepherd. Or I ask God a question like, "What does it mean that you make me lie down in green pastures and lead me beside quiet waters?" One night, God answered this long-asked question. It must have been the voice of the good shepherd who put this thought into my mind. The thought was this: "The 'green pastures' I make you lie down in" are when you come to the Bible and feed on my words. My habit is to read the Bible every morning and to read through the whole Bible every year. The 'quiet waters' God leads you to are also his words." I then realized that my time to read the Bible each day is early in the morning. Not lots of distractions; it's very quiet. Many times, I look forward to coming to read his word because I am upset or stressing about something. His words, as I sit in the quiet and think about them, often calm my spirit and give me peace of mind. The next verse in the Psalm says, "He restores my soul." Thank you, Lord!

At this point I must let you in on a personal struggle I am having right now as I am writing this. I am deeply troubled from being treated unfairly by a business I'm dealing with. A company I trusted failed to help me. I have negative thoughts about this situation. I cannot get them out of my mind. I try to turn it all over to God, but the troubling thoughts keep coming back. They torture me. I am so upset that I can't think. I begin to doubt my relationship with God even though I know I should be trusting Him. I try repeating Psalm 23 to get the disturbing thoughts out of my mind. But I can't even remember the words, so I cry out to God, "help me." I am in a battle for my mind to be at peace. I tell Satan, in Jesus' name, to leave me alone and that I belong to God.

WHO IS GOD? WHO AM I?

Finally, as I struggle to remember and repeat Psalm 23, the Spirit of God helps me. I remember it and I focus on the words "He leads me beside quiet waters." Then God brings another scripture to my mind. "In quietness and trust is your strength" (Isaiah 30:15). That word touches my heart. It gives me hope. I feel the darkness leaving my mind and now the peace of Christ Jesus is entering into me. I find myself in God's presence and I'm trusting Him. He will not fail me. He will show me the way and help me with the troubles that have been plaguing my mind and preventing His peace.

> Thank you Lord for coming to me in this battle for my mind, even questioning my faith in you. I really do want my heart to be in tune with your heart. I know I am your child and you love me and will help me. I was feeling out of touch with you and you came to me. Help me Lord to know what to do in this situation that has been overwhelming me. I want your will to be done in and through my life. Now I need your wisdom and guidance to know what to do. Thank you for quieting my mind and my heart. I know you will use this situation to grow me. I welcome you to change anything in my life so I can be more like you.

I think you get the point. Memorizing a scripture and slowing down to think about it changes our attitudes and keeps us in fellowship with God. It is one way to help us overcome our fears. When I was able to become calm, with God's help, I was able to sort out my feelings. I must now work through being discouraged and anxious, being hurt and angry, and fears of losing things I value. I am back on track. As Psalm 23:3 says, "He restores my soul." Restoration came because of memorizing and knowing God's word.

(2) PAY ATTENTION TO THE BIBLE'S "DO NOT FEAR" STATEMENTS. Prepare a list of "Do not fear" or "Fear not" verses from the Bible. When facing a fearful problem, read your list to be encouraged to know God is with you. By coming to believe the many scriptures where God says, "Do not fear, I am with you", I learn to trust that God really is with me. Besides Psalm 23:4, "Even though I walk

UNDERSTANDING AND APPLYING

through the valley of the shadow of death, I fear no evil, for You are with me...." Another one I often refer to is Isaiah 41:10. It is true, we overcome fear when we truly know God is with us. How do we learn and know that God is with us? Following are some ways I learn to trust God's presence in fearful situations.

(3) GET TO KNOW WHO GOD IS. We learn to know lots about God from reading about who He is in the Bible. Have you noticed there are times in the Bible where people reason with God and He listens to them. They know Him personally enough to be able to talk to Him like that. Thus, we see that a way to know God, apart from scripture, is to know God personally. Knowing God comes from seeing how He works in mine and others' lives. God works differently with different people. I've found that a great way to know God better is hearing from others how He has worked in their lives. Asking other people how God has helped them handle their fears helps me. Trusting God knows God well enough to know He will take care of you no matter what. He is a God I can trust. You can leave your burdens with Him and go your way in peace (Psalm 56:3-4, 11,13). Knowing God, and with His help, and the help of others, I now have very few times where fear overwhelms me. Praise be to God, whose living presence in our lives is our peace and security.

(4) KNOW HOW MUCH GOD CARES FOR YOU. We do this by reading stories in the Bible of how God is with people and cares about them. For me, God has shown Himself to be present many times throughout my life, and reviewing this has led me to remember, when faced with a fear, that God really does care about me (1 Peter 5:7). Make a list of things God has done for you that show you He cares for you. In the section earlier in this chapter, titled, FACTS THAT MAY HELP US OVERCOME A LACK OF PEACE WITH GOD, I shared a couple of examples of how I know God cares for me. Here is one other: My daughter and I had a garage sale to make a few dollars for a mission trip to South America. I sat in the driveway counting the money after the sale was over. We had $199.50. A thought came to me and I said to God, "God, if we had 50 cents more, we'd have $200 dollars even." At that moment a young boy came into the driveway and asked if he could buy something. I asked, "How much money do you have?" He said,

WHO IS GOD? WHO AM I?

"50 cents." I said, "You can have anything here for 50 cents." I'm sure you have stories like this. God cares even about little things in our lives. When tempted to be afraid, I use these, and other stories, to remind myself that "He cares for me." Why would I stop believing God cares for me when I see how many times, He has shown me His care?

(5) FACE YOUR FEARS BY NOT ALLOWING THEM TO CONTROL YOU. By doing things that I used to fear doing, I've learned that most fears are not true. Almost all of the fears we project don't happen. And if I project the worst thing that could happen, even then I know the future God promises me, and not even death can destroy that. So, I simply tell myself there is nothing to fear. And if there is, I believe God is with me to help me. I step out in faith and challenge my fear. I get up to check out a noise, or allow myself to ride airplanes, trusting and knowing that God is with me. Eventually, I lose the fear of things I used to fear.

(6) LEARN TO SENSE A COMING FEAR BEFORE IT GRABS YOU. When I feel fear rising up within me, I must learn to not let it enter my mind. Whenever I feel fear coming into my thinking, I dismiss it immediately, giving my issues over to God. I say to God, "I trust you", and then, by having learned that I can trust Him, I am able to dismiss those troubling thoughts before they get deeply rooted. Focusing on God instead of fear gives peace (Isaiah 26:3). Jesus even told us, "Do not let your heart be troubled" (John 14:1). The example I told you about in point one above was how I tried not to let my heart be troubled.

(7) ASK GOD TO GIVE YOU HIS PEACE. Sometimes, I have prayed, "God, I can't handle being anxious. Please, give me your peace." At times, God answered my prayer by flooding my heart with His peace (Psalm 34:4). Jesus promises to give us peace to calm our fearful hearts. In John 14:27, he was helping his disciples deal with the saddening fact that he would be killed and then leave them to go back to his Father in heaven. I believe he meant for us to know that his peace is available for other situations as well.

(8) TWO OTHER TRUTHS CONCERNING "BE NOT AFRAID." Truth one: At times God calls us to take a stand against evil, even if it means mistreatment and suffering. At other times Jesus says

to flee trouble. There are times to flee and hide (Consider Proverbs 28:28; John 8:59; Matthew 24:15-18). This does not mean we are cowards or that we lack bravery. We need God's wisdom to know when to choose between "flight or fight." God may want us to live to face another day so as to fulfill a purpose He has for us. Fear can serve as a protector, and sometimes protecting ourselves means to run away from physical danger. This is also true concerning moral temptations. At times, especially when tempted to do something wrong, we must flee. Joseph was an example when he ran away from the temptation to commit adultery (Genesis 39:1-12). Truth two: We may have physical or mental defects that are a result of the corruptions of nature. These defects may somehow be related to our feelings of fear. If so, recommended medications, or certain kinds of exercises, may correct the condition and would help one to better be able to deal with fears.

A CONCLUDING EXERCISE TO END THIS CHAPTER

This has been a long chapter with much information, perhaps too much for a mind to absorb it all. Sometimes an "overload" of the brain causes us to be confused. We need to step back and give what we have heard time to sink in. Eventually, the concepts become clearer, and we experience one of those "aah-ha" moments" that says, "Now I get it!" (Did I spell aah-ha right?) Here is an exercise to help you review the chapter and its meaning for your life.

Who is God?
After reading this chapter, one thing I have changed in my view about God is

_____
_____

Who am I?
What does it mean for you to live in the fear of the Lord always (Proverbs 23:17)?

_____
_____

WHO IS GOD? WHO AM I?

Did this chapter help me with my personal fears? How so, or why not?

_____

_____

_____

NEXT: THE FINAL CHAPTER

Next, we come to chapter ten, the final chapter of WHO IS GOD? WHO AM I? (A Guide to Unity in a Divided World) A JOURNEY LEADING TO LIFE (ABUNDANT AND ETERNAL). In chapter ten we shall focus on the subtitle of the book, "A Guide to Unity in a Divided World." It is no secret that we live in a very divided world. Even Christ's church is divided. Sadly, fear is one of the problems that causes many people not to trust the church. It is common for people to live their lives out of fear. One of the problems with fear is that it often leads to being a controlling person. A person controls things to be protected from getting hurt. Many leaders, whether in the world or in the church, do not recognize their fears, and therefore they try and control things to avoid what they fear. Unfortunately, our fears can hurt others and cause divisions. What can be done to bring Christ-honoring unity to the church and to the divided world in which we live? What are unifying factors in our relationships with each other, not only in the world, but especially in our Lord's church? Understanding and applying unifying factors to human relationships is how to create unity in diversity with people who differ from us in beliefs and lifestyles, but especially how to have unity in the diversified church of our Lord Jesus Christ. Chapter ten addresses these issues.

Chapter 10

UNDERSTANDING AND APPLYING UNIFYING FACTORS TO HUMAN RELATIONSHIPS.

BE OF ONE MIND, ACCEPT ONE ANOTHER AS CHRIST ACCEPTED US

Everywhere in our world we can observe angry feelings and division between people. How can we be united and loving with one another when we adamantly disagree about so many things? I speak especially to a divided church, of whom the Bible says this, "Now may the God who gives perseverance and encouragement grant you to be of the same mind with one another according to Christ Jesus, so that with one accord you may with one voice glorify the God and Father of our Lord Jesus Christ. Therefore, accept one another, just as Christ also accepted us to the glory of God" (Romans 15:5-7). This was written in the context of Romans 14 where God's people had difficulty accepting believers who differed from them.

The religious leaders in Jesus' day were to make God's temple a place where people could come to learn of God and worship Him. But those religious leaders would not accept certain people who differed from them, and they were not welcome in the temple. Jesus was not accepted because he hung out with unacceptable people. He was criticized by religious people for being a friend of sinners (Luke 5:29-32; 7:34, 36-50). Why did Jesus say he ate and spent time with sinners? Today, we are God's people, and we are the temple of God. Like those religious leaders, do we reject people who differ from our beliefs and lifestyles, or do we make people who differ from us feel accepted and loved?

At the beginning of this book, I stated the following as a primary purpose for the book. I said, "Unity in our personal lives and world is achieved by understanding and participating in diversity." Basically, this means discovering what factors lead to achieving unity with people

WHO IS GOD? WHO AM I?

in a diverse society. Accepting people is one of those unifying factors that leads to unity in relationships. In a moment, I will share an experience I once had with a woman who asked me a question. This woman's question illustrated for me a problem in the church and gave me an opportunity to help her understand some needed unifying factors. We in the church often have difficulty learning how to help people who differ with us to feel loved and accepted. One big reason is this. We think that if we accept them, we would be agreeing with their wrong beliefs and lifestyles. One way to achieve unity with people who differ from us is to help them feel accepted. We don't have to agree with people's lifestyles and beliefs to develop an acceptance of one another. This chapter will give some ways to do that. Why is this important, especially for Christians? Because accepting others is a vital ingredient for leading persons toward faith and wholeness in Christ.

HOW JESUS ADDRESSES THE ISSUE

Jesus spoke to this issue with His disciples when John, a disciple, said to Jesus, "Teacher, we saw someone casting out demons in Your name, and we tried to prevent him because he was not following us." But Jesus said, "Do not hinder him, for there is no one who will perform a miracle in My name, and be able soon afterward to speak evil of Me. For he who is not against us is for us" (Mark 9:38-40). Jesus made the point in verse 40 that we followers of Jesus must find common ground with others, even if they are not part of our circle. We must appreciate the need for oneness and unity with others outside our group who may be doing similar works for God that we are doing. Like Jesus said, "For whoever is not against us is for us." Rather than allowing ourselves as members of Christ's body to be divided over differing teachings and traditions, we must appreciate our joint efforts to spread the gospel. We must accept one another even as Christ has accepted us to the glory of God. This means moving toward unity in diversity.

Just before Jesus went to his death on the cross, what did he pray for all who would believe in Him? Here is what He prayed: "I do not ask on behalf of these alone, but for those also who believe in Me through their word; that they may all be one; even as You, Father, are in Me and I in You, that they also may be in Us, so that the world may believe that You sent Me. The glory which You have given Me I have given to them, that they may be one, just as We are one; I in them and You in Me, that they may be perfected in unity, so that the world may know that You sent Me, and loved them, even as You have loved Me… and I have made Your name known to them, and will make it known, so that the love with which You loved Me may be in them, and I in them." (John 17:20-23, 26). Jesus prayed that we, His church, would be one, unified, and loving with the love that God puts within us. We Christians need to have this mentality, even when we cannot agree over certain issues. Can we become the answer to Jesus' prayer for love and unity?

ONE WOMAN'S QUESTION IDENTIFIED THE PROBLEM

One day a woman approached me with a question. Her faith was upset because a friend who attended another church told her that a familiar verse of scripture meant something different than what she believed to be true. I could tell she felt shaken in her faith. Her question to me was, "Am I wrong to believe what I've believed? I've always believed that it was the truth." She wanted me to interpret the verse for her. She hoped I could settle the issue for her so that, instead of being confused and doubting, she could be sure she was believing the right thing in the Bible. This issue of what is right involves an ongoing problem in and among churches. Churches have differing doctrines that they hold dear. When I use the word "doctrine," I simply mean God's teachings about various subjects found in the Bible. A problem with insisting "we have the right view of the Bible, and you don't," is that it creates an "us versus them" mentality. This is an issue that divides today's church. Naturally, we all want to know and believe what the Bible says, and not what is false. After all, the truths of the Bible form the foundation of people's faith. But when differences occur, this often sets us up for an "I am right, you are wrong" mentality, bringing about confusion, doubt, and disunity.

WHO IS GOD? WHO AM I?
WHAT HAVE YOU OBSERVED?

Have you observed there is disunity and separation between people and churches over Bible doctrines? One example, which is only one of the doctrines churches disagree over, is the division in churches over what has come to be called "Calvinism" and "Arminianism." As a reformed pastor, John Calvin had good intentions in wanting people in the church to have absolute assurance of their salvation. He found his answer to help them gain assurance of their salvation in the Bible. Also, as a reformed pastor, Jacob Arminius had good intentions in not wanting people to leave the reformed church over doctrinal differences. Arminius respected Calvin and wanted to support him. Like Calvin, Arminius found his answer in the Bible that would help prevent people from leaving the church. Eventually, serious division was created in the church over the doctrines these men believed were true. I am not writing to support one of these over the other. Rather, my concern is to promote unity in spite of differences. Yes, the Bible expects us to believe in doctrinal truth, but the Bible also supports the doctrine of unity in the church. The apostle Paul writes in his letter to the Ephesian church, "…walk in a manner worthy of the calling with which you have been called, with all humility and gentleness, with patience, showing tolerance for one another in love, being diligent to preserve the unity of the Spirit in the bond of peace. There is one body and one Spirit, just as also you were called in one hope of your calling; one Lord, one faith, one baptism, one God and Father of all who is over all and through all and in all" (Ephesians 4:1-6). Thinking that unity is everyone believing the same thing, we can easily fail to understand what is needed to achieve unity in the midst of a diversity of beliefs. Notice in these verses a unifying factor in preserving unity in the bond of peace. That unifying factor is a person with the character traits of tolerance, patience, gentleness, and humility.

UNDERSTANDING AND APPLYING
FINDING COMMON GROUND IS A UNIFYING FACTOR

My aim in answering this woman's question was to help her with more than the issue as she perceived it. I not only wanted her to overcome upsetting doubts about her beliefs, but to also understand the problem of differences in churches and how to achieve unity. I pointed out to her that there are many differences in the church over what the Bible teaches. I explained that it is important to be open to talking about this with those who differ with us. It is helpful to listen to differing beliefs, not to argue, but to understand what is believed and why. In what way is this helpful? It is helpful because our goal is to see if we have things in common, especially, to see if we are fellow Christians, even though some of our beliefs may differ. By trying to understand the other person, we can discern whether or not they believe in Jesus as their savior, and if they believe the Bible is the word of God. It is important to know if we believe in the same Jesus and the same Bible. How can we know this? We can know by communicating and asking the right questions. One good question to ask is what they and their church are doing to fulfill Christ's great commission. You might find out they are doing some of the same things you and your church are doing to reach people for Christ. The more we can do to discover common ground, the more satisfied we are that they are a brother or sister in Christ. We need to keep asking questions and be open to listening and understanding their views. They may have some insight into the Bible and God's truth that we have missed. If so, we might want to give their scriptural viewpoint more thought. At the same time, we can share with them what we believe. This may help all involved to have a wider and improved understanding of Biblical teachings. In other words, since we differ in our doctrines which we base on the Bible, it might be good for us to be open to learn something we may have missed. An expanded knowledge could lead us to a more complete view of God's truth, leading us to a more balanced living of God's will.

Unfortunately, people, including you and me, can be so set in our faith, convinced that we are believing the right thing, that we will not be open to the possibility of another view being a part God's truth. I

WHO IS GOD? WHO AM I?

have found this is often the case. In our need to be right, it's easy to take parts of the Bible that do not seem to fit our view and try to make them fit what we want to believe. What can we do when we realize we do not agree? We can learn the areas where we do agree. We can find out whether or not they are following Jesus and seeking to do His will, and whether or not we are fellow Christians, looking to grow in our faith. If so, we can allow differences but still be one in love and in working together to reach people for Christ.

USING QUESTIONS TO REACH ACCEPTANCE AND GROWTH IN THE FAITH

How can we find out what others believe? We all have a theology; what is it? We can find out by asking questions. Following is a sample list of questions that we can ask. What do you believe about God and His miracles (Jonah 1:17, 2:10)? What do you believe about Jesus and Christianity being the only true religion (John 14:6; Acts 4:12)? What do you believe about how to become a Christian (Romans 10:8-17; John 3:16)? What do you believe about Christ's church (Matthew 16:18)? What do you believe about how God wants us to live, and why (Psalm 86:11)? What do you believe about the Bible (2 Timothy 3:16)? What do you believe about God's grace (Deuteronomy 30:15–20; Ephesians 2:8)? What do you believe about heaven and God committing people to hell (Matthew 10:28; Luke 12:4–5)? What do you believe about sin and its consequences (John 8:24)? What do you believe about God's judgment (Romans 14:10)? What do you believe about the trinity? What do you believe about what it means to be created in God's image (Genesis 1:27)? What do you believe about God's purpose for us (1 Peter 2:9)? What do you believe about God's salvation—past, present, and future (Philippians 3:20–21)? What do you believe about prayer (Luke 18:1)? What do you believe about how God wants us to relate to nonbelievers (Matthew 28:19-20; Galatians 6:10)? What do you believe about God creating the universe (Genesis 1:1)? What do you believe about what God is going to make happen in the future (Isaiah 13:9, 11–13; 2 Peter 3:13)? Why do you believe the things you believe about God? What truths do you believe must be

UNDERSTANDING AND APPLYING

agreed upon by all believers (Galatians 1:6-9)? Questions like these help us get to know one another's beliefs and heart toward God.

THE VALUE OF SHARING DIFFERENCES

Learning the differences between us and other believers does not mean we have to change what we believe. It simply means that their views may open doors to new insights into the Bible that we had not considered, and by you sharing your views, you may give them things to think about that they had not considered. From this exchange we may all grow in faith, maybe even change some of our beliefs if we are convinced it makes sense and is what the Bible really teaches. To learn more about the Bible from one another is a good thing and knowing that those who differ from us are also Christians with whom we have lots in common, goes a long way to helping us sense a oneness with one another, and a realized unity in Christ. This is part of the meaning of what unity in diversity is all about. We will be able to display peace with one another in the public eye, thus demonstrating our loving oneness in Christ (John 13:34-35). After making many of the above points with this woman who was shaken in her faith, I gave her two scriptures to apply to her situation.

USING ROMANS 14 AS A UNIFYING FACTOR

Romans 14 teaches us to have our own faith toward God, while allowing others the same grace. To help the woman I was talking with to be strengthened in her faith, I shared Romans 14:22 which says, "The faith which you have, have as your own conviction before God. Happy is he who does not condemn himself in what he approves." I assured the woman that if we believe our faith is based on God's word, we are not to condemn ourselves, nor let others condemn us for believing it. I wanted her to understand that what she believed was alright with God and that she can hold on to her beliefs, even if others differ. If a person sincerely believes God's word and is wanting to obey and serve God from the heart, then it is alright to believe what you believe because God is the ultimate one to whom we are responsible (see Romans 14:10-13). However, it is good to be open to change if God convinces us by the Holy Spirit concerning things in the scriptures that we had not seen before.

There is something else Romans 14 says: "Now accept the one who is weak in faith, but not for the purpose of passing judgment on his opinions. One person has faith that he may eat all things, but he who is weak eats vegetables only. The one who eats is not to regard with contempt the one who does not eat, and the one who does not eat is not to judge the one who eats, for God has accepted him. Who are you to judge the servant of another? To his own master he stands or falls; and he will stand, for the Lord is able to make him stand. One person regards one day above another, and another regards every day alike. Each person must be fully convinced in his own mind" (Romans 14:1-5). Even though this context speaks about eating or not eating meat sacrificed to idols, we can substitute our own areas of disagreement into the text. For example, here is a paraphrase of Romans 14:2-3: "the one who is Calvinistic, or Arminian is not to judge the one who is not Calvinistic or Arminian, for God has accepted him. Who are you to judge the servant of another? To his own master he stands of falls; and he will stand, for the Lord is able to make him stand." If we can think this way, unity in diversity can be reached.

ADOPTING THE MINDSET OF THE APOSTLE PAUL AS A UNIFYING FACTOR

In 1 Corinthians 1:10-12, we learn that the Corinthian church was a divided church. The believers were divided and quarrelling among themselves about who they should listen to. Paul, an apostle of Jesus, said to them,

> Let a man regard us in this manner, as servants of Christ and stewards of the mysteries of God. In this case, moreover, it is required of stewards that one be found trustworthy. But to me it is a very small thing that I may be examined by you, or by any human court; in fact, I do not even examine myself. For I am conscious of nothing against myself, yet I am not by this acquitted; but the one who examines me is the Lord.

UNDERSTANDING AND APPLYING

Therefore do not go on passing judgment before the time, but wait until the Lord comes who will both bring to light the things hidden in the darkness and disclose the motives of men's hearts; and then each man's praise will come to him from God (1 Corinthians 4:1-5).

We can adopt the same attitude and practice as Paul. Yes, it is good to discuss our differences with one another in hopes that we can add to a more complete understanding of God's word. But ultimately, as Paul writes, each of us is responsible to God for our own beliefs and practices. We are to realize that each of us has a calling from God and that God will be the final judge of our motives and ministry. The result of this mindset is that, instead of causing division from having an "I'm right you're wrong" mentality, we are to believe and do what we are convinced is God's will for us. What a blessing to be at peace with ourselves and with other believers, even if there are disagreements. God will sort things out in the end.

ANOTHER UNIFYING FACTOR IN ANY RELATIONSHIP IS THE USE OF OUR TONGUES

The Bible has much to say about how to use our voice in presenting things to others. We learn from James how difficult it is to control our tongues (James 3:1-10). That must be the reason there is so much in the Bible about how to wisely use our tongues in speaking to people. I'm talking about how to relate to people so that we have the opportunity and privilege to speak God's truth into their lives. Yes, there are times to rebuke others, or to not associate with others, but how we speak to them in gentleness, kindness and love can leave open doors for future input. We need God's wisdom to know how to speak to people in each situation we encounter. If we want to effectively reach people with the gospel of Jesus Christ, it is to our advantage to speak truth to them in a way they can accept, while at the same time maintaining open doors for future conversations.

The Bible has much to say about how to use our voice in saying things to others. Following are some of the Bible's teachings enabling us to use our tongues effectively. Many Proverbs remind us about how to speak wisely to others. For example, sometimes we may need to correct a person. The Bible says, "Like apples of gold in settings of silver is a word spoken in right circumstances. Like an earring of gold and an ornament of fine gold Is a wise reprover to a listening ear" (Proverbs 25:11-12). In other situations, we are told that our manner of speech makes a difference in how to gain a positive response from those we speak to. For example, "By forbearance a ruler may be persuaded, and a soft tongue breaks the bone" (Proverbs 25:15). Or "A gentle answer turns away wrath, but a harsh word stirs up anger. The tongue of the wise makes knowledge acceptable, but the mouth of fools spouts folly" (Proverbs 15:1-2). Also, notice the need for understanding a person before we speak, "He who gives an answer before he hears, it is folly and shame to him" (Proverbs 18:13). Thinking about and planning how to say things before we speak is also recommended. "The wise in heart will be called understanding, and sweetness of speech increases persuasiveness. Understanding is a fountain of life to one who has it, But the discipline of fools is folly. The heart of the wise instructs his mouth and adds persuasiveness to his lips. Pleasant words are a honeycomb, sweet to the soul and healing to the bones" (Proverbs 16:21-24). Consider the results if wisdom and kindness is in our voice. Here is a verse about thinking before we speak. "The heart of the righteous ponders how to answer, but the mouth of the wicked pours out evil things" (Proverbs 15:28). We need God's wisdom to know how to communicate rightly with people according to the situation.

This can be illustrated by the example of the person who was telling the woman I was speaking with that her belief was wrong. He was actually harming her instead of building her up. He may have had good intentions in wanting her to believe God's truth, but love is missing if it causes a fellow believer to unnecessarily stumble by creating doubt and guilt. Even if our theologies are correct, it does not always mean we are communicating them in a correct way when it comes to building loving relationships. One of the toughest things to live out as Christians is how to make people feel they are accepted, while at the same time not agreeing with their lifestyles or perceived misbeliefs. It is not true that if I accept them, I am enabling them to

UNDERSTANDING AND APPLYING

believe and do what is wrong. We can speak truth to them if we only knew how to speak the truth in a loving manner rather than in condescending judgment and condemnation. I believe in the need for right doctrine, but not in the misuse of right doctrine, for example, using it to as a power to control others due to our fears or having to be right. The truth is that Christians can learn how to bring about a unifying peace in the midst of a diversified world through the right use of their voice (Proverbs 16:7).

WHAT I AM NOT SAYING

Thus far in reading this chapter you may have thought of things that counter what I have been trying to say. After all, in discussing any subject, there is often a "yeah but…" side to consider. Following are comments that may address some of your thoughts of "what about this, or what about that."

1. I am not saying that whatever people want to believe from the Bible is okay. A lot of things in the Bible that we believe may be wrong, but there are some things in the Bible that we must get right because our eternal destiny is at stake. There is a heaven to gain and a hell to shun. Correct doctrine is vitally important when it comes to knowing how we receive eternal life (John 20:30-31). Many people will argue with family members or others over what is right and wrong, whether it's a belief or a practice in one's daily living. Here is a question to consider. Is your difference about these issues causing conflicts in your relationship? There is another issue deeper than whether or not it is right or wrong to do such and such. Instead of arguing over certain issues, you need to get at whether or not their belief or practice is keeping them out of heaven. Some things are not worth arguing about in light of the greater concern over how we get to heaven. That is the issue that needs to be addressed. Arguing over lesser issues may be keeping others from listening to you. So how do you address this issue with others? You can accept others, and at the same time ask questions. For example, you can ask, "Do you know that God has forgiven your sins?" and "How do you know that?" Those are fair questions, and they get at their deeper understanding about salvation. You could ask, "If

WHO IS GOD? WHO AM I?

you were to die tonight and meet St. Peter at the gates of heaven and he asks you, 'Why should I let you into heaven,' what would you say?" If their answer is something other than Jesus dying for their sins and belief in Him, then you know that whomever you are talking to needs to understand how to get to heaven. But how can you help them believe if you argue with them about how wrong they are. Is the death of Jesus on the cross a part of their beliefs? You can explore the meaning of that further with them, having a civil conversation. Do they honestly want to live for God? If so, in light of Romans 14, what is wrong with them believing something wrong, as long as they get God's way to salvation right? We will all stand before the judgment seat of Christ one day and all matters will be settled by Jesus. Let them have their beliefs, they may even change them once saved, but make sure they understand how to get to heaven.

2. I am not talking about accepting everyone's beliefs and lifestyles without being concerned about God's truth. There is much in the Bible about confronting people's sinful behaviors (Proverbs 24:23-26). And there are times when we need to be accountable to one another, with an attitude of being submissive to one another in the fear of Christ (Ephesians 5:21).

3. I am not saying that correct doctrines (Bible teachings) outside of salvation are unimportant and they don't matter. Correct understanding of the Bible's teachings is very important. God wants us to know the truth about Himself and about how to live our lives with a true faith, hope, and love. Many doctrines involve a study of the whole of Scripture, trying to put many pieces together. Accurately understanding a Bible doctrine can be a lifelong process of seeking to get it right. The Bible's teaching about the end times is one example. I often come away from reading my Bible with more questions than answers. That is why having a doctrinal belief that fails to consider opposing doctrines could be a problem; it could hold a piece we are missing. Here are three reasons that thinking "my doctrine is right, and your doctrine is wrong" can be dangerous. (1) If I do not have it right, at some point, an incorrect doctrine can cause us to live our Christian lives in an unbalanced, deficient, or harmful way. (2) Because of sin in our lives, we can unknowingly commit spiritual abuse by using our

"correct" theology to control others, guilting them into believing what we believe, or making them feel like ignorant or poor citizens in God's kingdom for not believing the "truth." (3) Thinking we have the final word about a particular doctrine and not being open to consider another side can prevent us from reading the Bible rightly because we think we already have it figured out. I have noticed that if something doesn't fit a person's understanding of scripture, they will work to make it fit with what they believe, rather than to be open to questioning or changing their view.

CONCLUSION

Here are personal questions for all of us to think about. (1) What if others besides myself are right in what they believe? Imagine yourself believing what they believe. Think about it. (2) How would believing what the other person believes affect your life? (3) How might it be good for me to believe it, or not good for me to believe it? Yes, it's okay to keep your beliefs. Yes, we must be able to refute those who contradict sound doctrine, even severely reprove those who are rebellious (Titus 1:9-16), but still, how we say things, when and where to say it, and what we say needs to be carefully constructed. Requirements for those who desire to be leaders in the church include not being argumentative, and to be gentle and peaceable" (1 Timothy 3:2-3). Discussing things with people, listening, and building relationships helps open the doors to speaking into their lives. And when we make mistakes and hurt others because of it, it is the beauty of our faith that we have forgiveness as the way to restoring peace and oneness between us. I hope that the comments in this chapter with the woman who asked me a question has helped her, and others, to see that we can be assured of our personal beliefs, while at the same time develop unity, love, and acceptance of persons with whom we differ. As Romans 14 instructs us, hold strongly to the faith as you presently understand it, but be open to change if the Holy Spirit gives you a truth not previously understood.

There are other things not included in this chapter concerning how to achieve unity amidst diversity. For example, the local church itself is made by God to be a unified diversity. Each person has his or her part

WHO IS GOD? WHO AM I?

to play in ministering to Christ's church. God has given each one of us a spiritual gifting to use for the building up of the body of Christ. I Corinthians 12 helps us see this, and unity grows as each person voluntarily practices what God wants him or her to do. Also, unity can be promoted through adult Bible classes where various doctrines of the Bible can be taught, where the people are given a chance to ask questions, and where fellow believers are allowed to honestly share views that differ, without being criticized or argued with. Hopefully, this chapter will open the door for giving further thought to the issue of how to achieve unity in the midst of diversity. To be sure, oneness, unity, and love won't happen among the wicked of the world who persist in lawlessness, but it needs to happen in the church. As one of the Proverbs says, "When a man's ways are pleasing to the LORD, He makes even his enemies to be at peace with him" (Proverbs 16:7). God made this world a diverse place and that is why there will always be diversity. A problem we all have is to learn how to walk in the ways of God that make for unity and peace.

Who is God? He is who He is. He said it of Himself; I AM WHO I AM" (Exodus 3:14). God is love, compassion, slow to anger, and forgiving. He is also a God of judgment, justice, and punishment (Exodus 34:6-7). It is not always easy to understand God, but if we look deeper, there are answers and ways that can help us accept God for who He is as revealed in His two books. Who am I? I am created to be in the image of God. I have gone away from God, but in Christ I am being restored to the image of God. I am not yet fully in His image, but I am in the process of knowing and loving Him and becoming like Him. Jesus is the exact image of God, and it is God's purpose for us to become like His Son (Romans 8:29). When Jesus comes to reign as King, that is when I will be fully restored and be like He is (Psalm 17:15; 1 Thessalonians 5:23-24; 1 John 3:1-3).

NEXT: Check out the Postscript. Where do we go from here?

POSTSCRIPT: WHERE DO WE GO FROM HERE?

Today's world seems to have gotten to the point where we cannot trust anyone. Most people I talk to these days see a world that has drastically changed. They see and admit that we live in a very divided and dangerous world, full of lies, deceit, and violence. In fact, this fearful thought enters many people's minds, "If the world keeps going the way it is, we will destroy ourselves." For believers in Christ Jesus, the expectation is that the second coming of Jesus must be soon. So, where do we go from here? How can we survive in a fear-filled world such as this, a world where it's hard to know the truth about anything?

It is a good thing to know that there are many in this generation who want to know the truth. They are looking for what will give them much needed and sought-after guidance. But where do they turn? Human governments are corrupt and divided. Greed controls even our health systems. Costs go up and there is so much divided opinion over the right foods to eat, the right drugs to take, and the best treatment for one's condition. We are being told that many things we trusted in the past can no longer be trusted. Many search the internet for reliable sources of help in knowing what's right, but what they find is differing opinions about everything. I think of Pilate, who interviewed Jesus before sentencing him to death on the cross (John 18:37-38). Jesus said to him, "I have come into the world, to testify to the truth. Everyone who is of the truth hears my voice." Pilate replied to Jesus, what many are saying today, "What is truth?"

Even spiritual sources of truth are hard to find. Many think churches cannot be trusted. What has caused people to think that? Well-known and highly respected church leaders have fallen into immorality or disfavor. Also, many Christians are hypocritical because they do not live by what they say they believe. When you read 1 Corinthians 1:10-12, doesn't it seem to you that today's church is divided for the same reason Paul said it was divided in his day? Paul criticized the church for lack of unity because they were following people rather than the truths of Christ. Some were following Paul, others Apollos, others Cephas, and others Jesus. Today it goes like this: We follow Augustine, we follow Luther, we follow Calvin, we follow Arminius, we follow

WHO IS GOD? WHO AM I?

Wesley, we follow Alexander Campbell, we follow Balthasar Hubmaier and the Anabaptist movement, we follow Mary Baker Eddy, we follow Ellen White, we follow Charles Taze Russell, we follow Joseph Smith, and on-and-on. The result is differing theologies, causing differing interpretations of the Bible, causing "we are right, and you are wrong" attitudes. Even though they all claim to follow Jesus, in the end there is a divided church, causing difficulty for anyone who is searching for who has the truth. No wonder there is confusion, not only in the world, but also in the church. The apostle Paul needed to help the church to be united by applying unifying principles that would bring them together in Christ Jesus. To help create unity in diversity he used teachings such as those in 1 Corinthians 4 and Romans 14 and 15.

Where do I turn? What can I trust to give me direction for how to successively live in the day in which we live? I said previously that Jesus is the key factor in bringing unity to a diversified world. I would say that Jesus and the Bible is still the best option for knowing God, His truth, and how to live in the today's world. I am not trying to steer you to a particular church, or person, but rather to the source of all things. That source of all things is the God who created us in His image, and whose two books provide us with a verifiable record of who He is and who we are.

God sent Jesus to be the savior of this world (1 John 4:14). We all need saving and this diverse world needs to be unified. Jesus and his teachings are what unifies us and everything else. If we are going to make a difference for good in this present world, we need to start by being remade in the image of God. That is why Romans 8:29 says that a primary goal of God for our lives is to become "conformed to the image of His son." Jesus, as a human, is the exact representation of who God is (Hebrews 1:3). Jesus said, "he who has seen me has seen the Father" (John 14:9). We were created to be in harmony with God, nature, others, and ourselves. Jesus is the one who restores the world to unity. If we want to have our lives restored and be involved in God's work of bringing unity to the world around us, we will do as Romans 13:14 says, we will "put on the Lord Jesus Christ." To put him on is to learn to be like him by following his example.

POSTSCRIPT

Jesus is God, who became a human like us (Philippians 2:6-7). This means he is now a man on the earth, and his Father is God in heaven. Jesus himself said many times, that as a human, he does nothing apart from the Father (John 5:19-20). What the Father does, he does. Jesus can do nothing on his own initiative. He does not seek his own will but always seeks the will of his Father (John 5:30; 6:38; Matthew 26:39). He speaks the things taught him by his Father (John 7:14-16; 8:28). Not only does he say what the Father tells him to say, but he obeys the Father (John 14:31). The Father knows Jesus, and Jesus knows the Father. They love each other. Jesus abides in the Father's love by keeping the Father's commandments. Jesus honors the Father (John 10:15; 15:10; 8:49). Jesus as human was in the image of God, that is, he exhibited all of the moral characteristics of God; love, patience, goodness, peace, and so forth (2 Corinthians 4:4; Hebrews 1:3).

How was Jesus enabled to do and say all the things he said and did? Where did he learn what God wanted him to do and speak? How did he have the strength to face all the tasks he had to do, even in the midst of opposition? Mark 1:35 says, "in the early morning while it was still dark, Jesus got up, left, and went away to a secluded place, and prayed there." Luke 6:12 says on another occasion, "he went off to the mountain to pray, and he spent the whole night in prayer to God." Other verses speak of his prayer life (Luke 5:16; 9:28-29; Matthew 14:23). John 17 is a whole chapter letting us in on one of his prayers. In the flesh, as a son of God, he offered up prayers to the Father with loud crying and tears to the one who could save him from death, and he learned obedience from the things he suffered (Hebrews 5:7-8). Jesus got through life and learned God's will for him by getting alone with his Father and meeting with Him in times of conversation on a regular basis. I suspect that his disciples asked him to teach them how to pray because they saw how important it was to him, and they noticed the amazing things he said and did. Could it be that Jesus' intimate relationship with the Father was the secret to his strength and power to live a godly life? Are we to take our cue from him and relate to God the Father as he did, relying totally on the Father?

WHO IS GOD? WHO AM I?

How then do we become like Jesus? If we want to become like Jesus, we must hang out with him. By seeing how Jesus hung out with his Father, and by seeing how this enabled him to make a difference for good in this world, we likewise are to follow Jesus' example so that we too can be who God created us to be and make a difference for good in this world. It is like I said at the very beginning of this book, "Unity in our personal lives and world is achieved by understanding and participating in diversity." This happens when we are connected with Jesus, for he is the ultimate restorer of the unity of all things (Acts 3:17-19; Colossians 1:15-17).

Who am I? Like Jesus, as his follower, I too love God and He loves me. I too want to honor God with my obedience. I too need to get away often and commune with God to learn from Him what His will is for my life. He speaks to me through His word, the Bible. I commune with Him when I talk to Him about His words to me, and about how I am feeling, and about what I need each day to help me live a right life. I too am to gain strength from those times of personal communion. It is during those times that I learn who God is and who I am. There are many things I absolutely need to receive from spending time with our Father, just as he got from times he spent time with his Father. Such is the primary purpose of this book. To slow down, take time to be with God, and focus on what his word is saying about who God is and who I am. That is what will satisfy us and make us to be in unity and oneness with God, nature, and each other. That is where we go from here.

"Before refrigerators were invented, people used ice houses to preserve their food. During the winter, people cut large blocks of ice from the frozen lakes and streams. They hauled them to the ice houses and covered them with sawdust so the ice wouldn't melt. The story is told of one man who lost a valuable watch while working in an ice house. He searched diligently for it by carefully raking through the sawdust. But he didn't find it. Other people also looked for the watch, but they didn't find it either. One day a small boy slipped into the ice house during the noon hour. After a few minutes, he came out with the watch in his hand. Amazed, the men asked him how he found it. "It was simple," the boy replied. "I just closed the door, lay down in the sawdust, and kept very still. Soon I heard the watch ticking." Like the

POSTSCRIPT

men who couldn't find the watch because they weren't listening, many of us fail to hear God speak because we are too busy and distracted to be listening.[19]

Jesus got alone with God and heard God speak to him. Was Isaiah referring to Jesus when he wrote, "The Lord GOD has given Me the tongue of disciples, that I may know how to sustain the weary one with a word. He awakens Me morning by morning, He awakens My ear to listen as a disciple" (Isaiah 50:4). Can we do that? Jesus said, "My sheep hear My voice, and I know them, and they follow Me" (John 10:27). How do we listen so we can hear from God? Many faithful Christians have learned how to practice listening to God. If you are interested, many articles can be read on the internet from persons who have learned to do this. Type in "listening prayer" and many articles should show up.

In this book, the times you take to read the scriptures and do the projects are meant to help you hear from God. Remember, we are not to be simply hearers of the word, but doers as well (James 1:19-25). Remember also, it is often true, we become like those with whom we spend the most time.[20]

---

19 This story is from a sermon, "Listening to the Sounds of Silence", by Steven Boersma, Aug. 6, 2012

20 I came across a book in a used bookstore that I bought because it discussed an issue I want to improve in my own life. It is about the importance of spending time with God, how to do it, and the value of doing it. Her book's subtitle is "Finding intimacy with God through a daily devotional life." You may have heard her on a daily radio program. Nancy Leigh DeMoss, "A Place of Quiet Rest" (Moody Press, Chicago), 2000.

SCRIPTURE INDEX

1

1 Corinthians 1:10-12 --------------148, 155
1 Corinthians 1:2 ---------------------------70
1 Corinthians 10:31 -------------------------58
1 Corinthians 10:6-11 -----------------------29
1 Corinthians 11:3--------------------------50
1 Corinthians 12:12-26----------------------49
1 Corinthians 13:4-7 ------------------------48
1 Corinthians 13:4-8 ------------------------47
1 Corinthians 15:12-22----------------------43
1 Corinthians 15:1-4 ------------------------77
1 Corinthians 15:26 -------------------------43
1 Corinthians 15:42-44----------------------91
1 Corinthians 15:45-49----------------------66
1 Corinthians 15:50-54----------------------89
1 Corinthians 2:10-11 -----------------------35
1 Corinthians 2:9 ---------------------------89
1 Corinthians 3:12-15 -----------------------90
1 Corinthians 3:9 ---------------------------55
1 Corinthians 4-------------------------- 156
1 Corinthians 4:1-5------------------- 54, 149
1 Corinthians 4:7 ---------------------------49
1 Corinthians 5:9-10 ------------------------84
1 Corinthians 5:9-13 ------------------------83
1 Corinthians 6:2-3-------------------------91
1 Corinthians 8:6 ---------------------------34
1 John 1:1-2--------------------------------95
1 John 1:1-3--------------------------------95
1 John 2:15---------------------------------84
1 John 2:15-17 -----------------------------84
1 John 2:16---------------------------------85
1 John 2:1-6------------------------------ 122
1 John 2:1-6; 3:2-10 ---------------------- 130
1 John 2:17-----------------------------54, 84
1 John 2:25, 29--------------------------- 106
1 John 2:3-6------------------------------ 106
1 John 3:1-3--------------------------123, 154
1 John 3:1-6------------------------------ 115
1 John 4:13------------------------------- 107

1 John 4:14---------------------------- 55, 156
1 John 4:15-19 ------------------------------90
1 John 4:16---------------------------------79
1 John 4:18------------------------------- 132
1 John 4:19---------------------------------47
1 John 4:19-21 ------------------------------81
1 John 4:7-11 ----------------------------- 106
1 John 4:8 ---------------------------------47
1 John 5:11-13 --------------------------- 105
1 Kings 11:1-6 ------------------------------46
1 Kings 22:19-22 ----------------------------32
1 Peter 1:1-11 ---------------------------- 117
1 Peter 1:14-16---------------------------- 115
1 Peter 1:3 ---------------------------------88
1 Peter 1:3-4 -------------------------------88
1 Peter 1:3-5 -------------------------------57
1 Peter 1:3-9 ------------------------------ 107
1 Peter 2:24 --------------------------------89
1 Peter 2:9 ------------------------------- 146
1 Peter 4:1-2 -------------------------------54
1 Peter 5:6-7 -------------------------------25
1 Peter 5:7 ------------------------------- 137
1 Peter. 5:7 ------------------------------ 124
1 Samuel 15:24-29 --------------------------54
1 Samuel 16:7 ------------------------------53
1 Samuel 17:23-24 ------------------------ 132
1 Thessalonians 2:13 ------------------------27
1 Thessalonians 4:13-18 --------------------91
1 Thessalonians 4:16-18 --------------------43
1 Thessalonians 5:18 ------------------------58
1 Thessalonians 5:23-24 ------------------ 154
1 Timothy 1:5-------------------------------90
1 Timothy 2:13-14---------------------------63
1 Timothy 3:2-3 --------------------------- 153
1 Timothy 5:20------------------------------83
1 Timothy 6:17-19---------------------------88

2

2 Chronicles 15:1-6 -------------------------28
2 Corinthians 1:3-4; -------------------------57

WHO IS GOD? WHO AM I?

2 Corinthians 10:5 — 45
2 Corinthians 11:3 — 63
2 Corinthians 13:5 — 106, 122
2 Corinthians 3:17 — 34
2 Corinthians 4:4 — 157
2 Corinthians 5:10 — 89, 118
2 Corinthians 5:10-11 — 114
2 Corinthians 5:14-15 — 115
2 Corinthians 5:17 — 47, 84, 107
2 Corinthians 5:9-10 — 122
2 Corinthians 7:1 — 115
2 Kings 18:28-35 — 16
2 Kings 19:14-20; 32-37 — 17
2 Kings 19:15 — 31
2 Peter 1:21 — 34
2 Peter 1:4 — 98
2 Peter 3:13 — 146
2 Peter 3:9 — 72, 118
2 Samuel 12:23 — 91
2 Thessalonians 1:5-9 — 118
2 Thessalonians 1:6-8 — 113
2 Timothy 2:21-26 — 83
2 Timothy 3:14-17 — 19
2 Timothy 3:1-5 — 72, 123
2 Timothy 3:16 — 146
28:28 — 139

A

Acts 1:6-11 — 90
Acts 10:34-35 — 117
Acts 10:38 — 47, 88
Acts 14:15 — 31
Acts 14:15-17 — 128
Acts 17:22-31 — 15, 37
Acts 17:24 — 31
Acts 17:24-28 — 31
Acts 17:26-34 — 129
Acts 17:30-31 — 118
Acts 18:9-10 — 132
Acts 20:35 — 88
Acts 27:14-17 — 132
Acts 3:17-19 — 158
Acts 3:17-21 — 118
Acts 3:19-21 — 89

Acts 4:12 — 146
Acts 4:25-26 — 34
Acts 4:32-35 — 82
Amos 7:1-6 — 54
Amos 8:11-12 — 27

C

Colossians 1:13 — 84
Colossians 1:13-14 — 108
Colossians 1:15-17 — 158
Colossians 1:16-17 — 33
Colossians 3:21 — 89
Colossians 3:23-24 — 88, 89

D

Daniel 7:13-14 — 90
Deuteronomy 10:20 — 67
Deuteronomy 17:14-20 — 46
Deuteronomy 17:18-20 — 128
Deuteronomy 30:11-20 — 130
Deuteronomy 30:15–20 — 146
Deuteronomy 31:11-13 — 128
Deuteronomy 31:24-26 — 19
Deuteronomy 33:27 — 31
Deuteronomy 5:1-33 — 55
Deuteronomy 5:29 — 84, 122
Deuteronomy 5:32-33 — 55
Deuteronomy 6:16 — 67
Deuteronomy 6:4 — 35
Deuteronomy 8:2-3 — 66
Deuteronomy 8:3 — 66

E

Ecclesiastes 12:13 — 112
Ecclesiastes 3:11 — 43
Ecclesiastes 3:12-14 — 131
Ephesians 1:13 — 104
Ephesians 1:13-14 — 117
Ephesians 1:3-7 — 79
Ephesians 2:1, 5 — 34
Ephesians 2:1-10 — 64
Ephesians 2:1-3 — 65

SCRIPTURE INDEX

Ephesians 2:1-5, 12 — 97
Ephesians 2:19 — 84
Ephesians 2:8 — 146
Ephesians 4:1-6 — 144
Ephesians 4:17-19 — 122
Ephesians 4:22-24 — 80, 85
Ephesians 4:7-16 — 49
Ephesians 5:21 — 54, 152
Ephesians 5:8-10 — 39
Exodus 1:17-21 — 115
Exodus 14:30-31 — 112, 116, 128
Exodus 19:16-25 — 113
Exodus 20:1-17 — 55
Exodus 20:18-20 — 113
Exodus 20:7 — 57
Exodus 3:14 — 154
Exodus 32:9-14 — 54
Exodus 34:6-7 — 75, 112, 115, 154
Ezekiel 11:19-20 — 47
Ezekiel 14:14, 20 — 71
Ezekiel 18:23 — 118
Ezekiel 18:23, 32 — 71, 72
Ezekiel 20:8-17 — 57
Ezekiel 34:25 — 45
Ezekiel 36:24-27 — 84
Ezekiel 36:24-28 — 117
Ezekiel 36:26-27 — 56, 107

G

Galatians 1:3-4 — 55
Galatians 1:4 — 98
Galatians 1:6-9 — 147
Galatians 3:2, 14 — 104
Galatians 3:28 — 50
Galatians 5:16-23 — 56
Galatians 5:19-21 — 123
Galatians 6:10 — 146
Galatians 6:9 — 88
Genesis 1:1 — 31, 38, 93, 146
Genesis 1:1-2 — 71
Genesis 1:1-3, 21, 27 — 36
Genesis 1:14-18 — 36
Genesis 1:2 — 33
Genesis 1:2, 31 — 37
Genesis 1:22 — 36
Genesis 1:26 — 32, 33, 38
Genesis 1:26-27 — 36
Genesis 1:26-28 — 37, 41
Genesis 1:27 — 146
Genesis 1:3, 6, 9 — 36
Genesis 1:31 — 26, 36
Genesis 1:3-5, 9, 24, 21-22, 26-28 — 36
Genesis 15:16 — 118
Genesis 15:1-6 — 119
Genesis 18:23-25 — 118
Genesis 19:1-16 — 130
Genesis 2:15-17 — 96
Genesis 2:16-17 — 37, 43, 45, 96
Genesis 2:18 — 41
Genesis 2:22 — 41
Genesis 2:22-24 — 64
Genesis 2:23 — 41
Genesis 2:24 — 41
Genesis 2:7 — 11, 41, 43, 107
Genesis 2:7; 7:22 — 33
Genesis 20:1-11 — 130
Genesis 21:16-17 — 132
Genesis 22:1-2, 12 — 66
Genesis 3:10 — 132
Genesis 3:1-13 — 63
Genesis 3:1-24 — 62, 76
Genesis 3:14-24 — 68
Genesis 3:15 — 70
Genesis 3:17-19 — 70
Genesis 3:21 — 79, 85
Genesis 3:22 — 33
Genesis 3:6 — 63
Genesis 3:6, 9-10 — 96
Genesis 3:7 — 64
Genesis 39:1-12 — 139
Genesis 4:1-16 — 68
Genesis 4:25-26 — 70
Genesis 4:26 — 70
Genesis 4:3-15 — 133
Genesis 5:1-32 — 70
Genesis 5:21-24 — 70
Genesis 5:24 — 70
Genesis 5:28-32 — 70
Genesis 50:18-21 — 132

WHO IS GOD? WHO AM I?

Genesis 6:22 — 71
Genesis 6:3 — 71
Genesis 6:5-6 — 118
Genesis 6:5-8 — 70
Genesis 6:8-9 — 71
Genesis 6:9 — 70

H

Hebrews 1:1-2 — 19
Hebrews 1:2 — 33
Hebrews 1:2-3 — 42
Hebrews 1:3 — 156, 157
Hebrews 10:26-31 — 114
Hebrews 11:17-19 — 124
Hebrews 11:31 — 130
Hebrews 11:6 — 28, 117, 126
Hebrews 11:7 — 71
Hebrews 12:3-11 — 123
Hebrews 12:4-11 — 130
Hebrews 13:6 — 132
Hebrews 2:15 — 132
Hebrews 4:1-7 — 74
Hebrews 5:7-8 — 157

I

I Corinthians 12 — 154
I John 4:16-18 — 121
Isaiah 1:16-17 — 82
Isaiah 11:2 — 34
Isaiah 13:9 — 146
Isaiah 13:9-11 — 73
Isaiah 14:21-27 — 55
Isaiah 26:3 — 138
Isaiah 30:15 — 136
Isaiah 41:10 — 137
Isaiah 43:10 — 31
Isaiah 43:10b-11 — 93, 94
Isaiah 43:25 — 98
Isaiah 43:6-7 — 57
Isaiah 44:24 — 31
Isaiah 44:6-8; 45:5, 21-22 — 32
Isaiah 45:18 — 23, 44
Isaiah 5:20 — 5

Isaiah 50:4 — 159
Isaiah 55:1-3, 7 — 118
Isaiah 61:10 — 85
Isaiah 65:1-25 — 119
Isaiah 65:17 — 118
Isaiah 65:17; 66:22 — 89
Isaiah 65:17-25 — 90
Isaiah. 6:1-5 — 114

J

James 1:17-18 — 57
James 1:19-25 — 159
James 2:5 — 88
James 3:1-10 — 149
James 4:6 — 58
James 5:10-11 — 71
Jeremiah 10:11 — 32
Jeremiah 26:12-13 — 54
Jeremiah 32:36-42 — 124
Jeremiah 34:12-17 — 57
Jeremiah 8:18-22 — 46, 118
Job 1:1 — 71
Job 1:1, 8 — 112
Job 1:1; 2:3 — 130
Job 1:6-12; 2:1-6; 38:4-7 — 32
Job 19:25-27 — 34, 43, 71
Job 32:1-10 — 34
Job 32-37 — 34
Job 33:4 — 34
Job 34:14-15 — 34
Job 38:3-7 — 31
Job 40:15 — 71
Job 42:7 — 34
Joel 2:13 — 75, 112
John 1:10-13 — 103
John 1:1-3 — 33
John 1:14 — 33
John 1:34 — 33
John 10:15 — 157
John 10:27 — 159
John 10:9-10 — 21
John 11:25-26 — 101
John 12:24-25 — 81
John 13:34-35 — 88, 147

164

SCRIPTURE INDEX

John 13:35 —————————————47
John 14:1-3 ————————————— 108
John 14:15 —————————————58
John 14:20 ————————————— 102
John 14:26; 15:26 ————————————34
John 14:27 ————————————— 138
John 14:31 ————————————— 47, 157
John 14:6 ————————————— 21, 83, 146
John 14:8-9 —————————————42
John 14:9 ————————————— 16, 59, 156
John 14:9-12; 17:4-5————————————82
John 15:12 —————————————47
John 17 ————————————— 157
John 17: 14-16 —————————————84
John 17:20-21 —————————————54
John 17:20-23, 26 ————————————— 143
John 17:22 ————————————— 102
John 17:3 —————————————88, 95
John 18:36 —————————————84
John 18:37-38 ————————————— 155
John 20:30-31 ————————————— 151
John 3:1-3 —————————————57
John 3:14-16 ————————————— 100
John 3:16 —————————————117, 118
John 3:16-18 —————————————73
John 3:19-20 ————————————— 132
John 3:36 ————————————— 65, 83, 113
John 3:3-6 —————————————84
John 3:3-8 ————————————— 103
John 3:5-6; 6:63 —————————————33
John 4:14 —————————————92
John 4:16-18 ————————————— 124
John 4:24 —————————————34, 41
John 5:19-20 ————————————— 157
John 5:24 ————————————— 108
John 5:30 ————————————— 157
John 5:30; 6:38; 14:28; 15:10 ————————51
John 6: 66-69 ————————————— 100
John 7:14-16 ————————————— 157
John 7:24 —————————————47
John 7:37-39 ————————————— 118
John 8:24 ————————————— 146
John 8:44 —————————————63
John 8:59 ————————————— 139
John 9:1-41 ————————————— 120

Jonah 1:17, 2:10 ————————————— 146
Jonah 3:10—————————————54
Jonah 3:3-10 ————————————— 128
Jonah 4:2 ————————————— 112
Joshua 2 ————————————— 129
Joshua 2:1-14————————————— 130
Joshua 2:1-21 ————————————— 117
Joshua 22:25————————————— 129
Joshua 23:16————————————— 123
Joshua 24:14-20 ————————————— 129
Jude 1:14-16 —————————————70

L

Leviticus 19:2 ————————————— 130
Luke 10:17-20 —————————————88
Luke 10:9 —————————————88
Luke 12:4-5—————————————73
Luke 12:4–5————————————— 146
Luke 13:1-5—————————————83
Luke 16:15—————————————53
Luke 18:1 ————————————— 146
Luke 18:26-27 —————————————64
Luke 19:41-44 ————————————— 118
Luke 2:10-11 —————————————75
Luke 21:25-26 ————————————— 132
Luke 24:36-39 ————————————— 114
Luke 24:37-39 —————————————89
Luke 24:39—————————————41
Luke 5:16 ————————————— 157
Luke 5:29-32; 7:34, 36-50 ———————— 141
Luke 5:4-8 ————————————— 114
Luke 6:12 ————————————— 157
Luke 6:40 —————————————29
Luke 8:22-25 ————————————— 124
Luke 8:52-55 —————————————42
Luke 9:22-24 —————————————81
Luke 9:23-24 —————————————58

M

Mark 1:14-15 —————————————87
Mark 1:35 ————————————— 157
Mark 1:8 ————————————— 104
Mark 10:17-22 —————————————94

WHO IS GOD? WHO AM I?

Mark 10:18 — 62
Mark 10:44-45 — 54
Mark 4:36-41 — 114
Mark 4:37-39 — 132
Mark 4:40 — 133
Mark 9:38-40 — 142
Matthew 10:28 — 146
Matthew 10:42 — 90
Matthew 10:7 — 88
Matthew 11:28-30 — 128
Matthew 14:23 — 157
Matthew 14:28-31 — 122
Matthew 16:18 — 146
Matthew 18:3 — 84
Matthew 19:27-28 — 91
Matthew 19:29 — 88
Matthew 22:36-39 — 47
Matthew 24:12 — 72
Matthew 24:15-18 — 139
Matthew 24:42-47; 25:14-21 — 91
Matthew 24:9-13, 21-22 — 56
Matthew 25:34 — 88
Matthew 26:39 — 157
Matthew 28:19 — 35
Matthew 28:19-20 — 146
Matthew 4:1-10 — 66
Matthew 4:17 — 87
Matthew 5:5 — 89, 131
Matthew 6:10 — 90
Matthew 6:14-15 — 47
Matthew 6:25, 34 — 132
Matthew 6:26 — 45
Matthew 6:26-32 — 23
Matthew 6:33 — 88
Matthew 6:9 — 57
Matthew 6:9-13 — 57
Matthew 7:11 — 58
Matthew 7:1-5 — 47
Matthew 7:21 — 54
Matthew 8:11 — 91
Matthew. 5:48 — 16
Micah 3:8 — 35
Micah 4:1-3 — 90
Micah 6:8 — 82

N

Nahum 1:3 — 112
Nehemiah 9:17 — 75
Numbers 11:25, 29 — 35
Numbers 15:27-31 — 130

P

Philippians 1:6 — 87
Philippians 2:3-11 — 54
Philippians 2:6-7 — 157
Philippians 3:20 — 91
Philippians 3:20-21 — 108
Philippians 3:20–21 — 146
Philippians 3:7-11 — 85
Philippians 3:7-9 — 119
Proverbs 1:22 — 127
Proverbs 1:23-31 — 128
Proverbs 1:29 — 129
Proverbs 1:29-33 — 112
Proverbs 1:5 — 127
Proverbs 1:7 — 127, 131
Proverbs 1:7; 9:10 — 112
Proverbs 10: 2, 16, 24 — 120
Proverbs 15:1-2 — 150
Proverbs 15:28 — 150
Proverbs 16:21-24 — 150
Proverbs 16:7 — 151, 154
Proverbs 17:11 — 117
Proverbs 17:3 — 124
Proverbs 18:10 — 119
Proverbs 18:13 — 150
Proverbs 19:23 — 112, 131
Proverbs 2:5-15 — 112
Proverbs 21:2 — 53
Proverbs 23:17 — 139
Proverbs 23:17-18 — 124
Proverbs 24:23-26 — 152
Proverbs 25:11-12 — 150
Proverbs 25:15 — 150
Proverbs 27:17; 15 — 29
Proverbs 28:13 — 132
Proverbs 28:14 — 113
Proverbs 29:1 — 72, 113

SCRIPTURE INDEX

Proverbs 3:13-15 — 46
Proverbs 3:7; 16:6 — 112
Proverbs 30:8-9 — 58
Proverbs 6:6 — 45
Proverbs 6:6-11 — 25
Proverbs 8:13 — 112
Proverbs 8:32 — 127
Proverbs 9:10 — 127
Proverbs 9:4-6 — 128
Psalm 102:25-26 — 85, 89
Psalm 102:25-27 — 93
Psalm 104:30 — 33
Psalm 110:1-3 — 91
Psalm 112:1-6 — 112
Psalm 115:16 — 44
Psalm 116:12-17 — 70
Psalm 119 — 26
Psalm 17:15 — 154
Psalm 17:3 — 124
Psalm 19 — 26
Psalm 19:1 — 23
Psalm 19:11-13 — 26
Psalm 19:1-6 — 23, 26
Psalm 19:4-6 — 23
Psalm 19:7-14 — 26
Psalm 19:7-9 — 26
Psalm 2 — 34
Psalm 2:7-8 — 67
Psalm 23 — 135, 136
Psalm 23:1-6 — 135
Psalm 23:3 — 136
Psalm 23:4 — 57, 136
PSALM 25 — 56
Psalm 25:1-3 — 56
Psalm 33:16-17 — 46
Psalm 33:8 — 112
Psalm 34:4 — 138
Psalm 40:11 — 75
Psalm 46:2-3 — 132
Psalm 5:4 — 45
Psalm 51:11 — 34
Psalm 56:3-4, 11,13 — 137
Psalm 66 — 120
Psalm 82 — 32
Psalm 86:11 — 112, 146
Psalm 9:8 — 118
Psalm 90:2 — 31, 93
Psalm 91:11-12 — 66
Psalm. 24:1 — 44

R

Revelation 12:9 — 63
Revelation 20:11-15 — 73, 89
Revelation 20:12 — 118
Revelation 21:3-4 — 88
Revelation 21:4-5 — 91
Revelation 21:4-7 — 131
Revelation 22:12 — 118
Revelation 3:20 — 96
Revelation 4:11 — 31
Revelation 5:9-10 — 90
Revelation 6:12-17 — 113
Roman 13:1-7 — 51
Romans 1:16 — 77
Romans 1:18-21 — 23
Romans 1:18-25 — 15
Romans 1:18-32 — 128
Romans 1:19-20 — 19
Romans 1:20 — 23, 24
Romans 1:28-32 — 123
Romans 10:13-15 — 104
Romans 10:8-17 — 146
Romans 12:2 — 84
Romans 12:21 — 45, 120
Romans 13:1-2 — 50
Romans 13:14 — 156
Romans 13:3-4 — 132
Romans 14 — 152, 153
Romans 14 and 15 — 156
Romans 14:10 — 146
Romans 14:10-13 — 147
Romans 14:1-5 — 148
Romans 14:17 — 88
Romans 14:22 — 147
Romans 14:2-3 — 148
Romans 15:5-7 — 141
Romans 2:1-6 — 47
Romans 2:4 — 83, 128
Romans 2:4-5 — 117

WHO IS GOD? WHO AM I?

Romans 4:13 ------------------------- 89, 131
Romans 4:1-8 -------------------------------- 85
Romans 4:5-8 -------------------------------- 89
Romans 5:1 --------------------------------- 121
Romans 5:12 --------------------------------- 43
Romans 5:12-21 ----------------------------- 64
Romans 5:14 --------------------------------- 66
Romans 5:8-9 ---------------------- 77, 98, 101
Romans 6:1-14 ----------------------------- 130
Romans 6:23 ---------------------------- 77, 99
Romans 7:18-24 ----------------------------- 68
Romans 7:21 --------------------------------- 77
Romans 7:24 --------------------------------- 77
Romans 8:1 ---------------------------------- 89
Romans 8:11 ---------------------------- 55, 89
Romans 8:1-4 -------------------------------- 48
Romans 8:16-17 ----------------------------- 89

Romans 8:20-21 ------------------------- 62, 68
Romans 8:28-29 ------------------------- 42, 81
Romans 8:29 ---------------- 16, 86, 154, 156
Romans 8:31-39 --------------------------- 123
Romans 8:32 --------------------------------- 58
Romans 8:5-13 ------------------------------- 47
Romans 8:9-11 -------------- 34, 43, 48, 104

T

Titus 1:9-16 -------------------------------- 153
Titus 2:11-14, 3:14 ------------------------- 88

Z

Zechariah 14:1-9 ---------------------------- 90
Zechariah 4:6 -------------------------------- 39

www.ingramcontent.com/pod-product-compliance
Lightning Source LLC
Chambersburg PA
CBHW072200070526
44585CB00015B/1223